# Problem Solving Workbook

## with Reading Strategies

Harcourt Brace & Company
Orlando • Atlanta • Austin • Boston • San Francisco • Chicago • Dallas • New York • Toronto • London
*http://www.hbschool.com*

Printed in the United States of America

ISBN 0-15-311095-3

9 10 11 12 13 14 15 16 082 2005 2004 2003 2002 2001

# CONTENTS

## Getting Ready for Grade 1



## CHAPTER 1 Understanding Addition



## CHAPTER 2 Understanding Subtraction



## CHAPTER 3 Addition Combinations



## CHAPTER 4 Addition Facts to 10



## CHAPTER 5 Subtraction Combinations



## CHAPTER 6 Subtraction Facts to 10



## CHAPTER 7 Solid Figures



## CHAPTER 8 Plane Figures

## CHAPTER 19 Telling Time



## CHAPTER 20 Measuring Length



## CHAPTER 21 Measuring Mass, Capacity, and Temperature



## CHAPTER 22 Fractions



## CHAPTER 23 Organizing Data



## CHAPTER 24 Making Graphs



## CHAPTER 25 Facts to 18



## CHAPTER 26 More About Facts to 18



## CHAPTER 27 Multiply and Divide



## CHAPTER 28 Two-Digit Addition and Subtraction

Name ____________________

# One-to-One Correspondence

1.

2.

3.

4.

Choose the best hat.
Draw one hat for each person.

Name ______________________________



# More and Fewer

1.

2.

Draw more windows on the house.
Draw fewer windows on the house.

Name ____________________



# Numbers Through 5

Count how many objects
each person is juggling.
Write the number of objects.

Name ______________________________



# Numbers Through 9

Count how many of each.
Write the number.

Name ______________________________



# Ten

| | Guess | Check |
|---|---|---|
| (turtle) | | |

| | Guess | Check |
|---|---|---|
| (fish) | | |

| | Guess | Check |
|---|---|---|
| (water lily) | | |

| | Guess | Check |
|---|---|---|
| (frog) | | |

Guess how many of each.
Then count to check your answer.

Name ____________________



# Greater Than

| | | Inside | Outside |
|---|---|---|---|
| 1. | 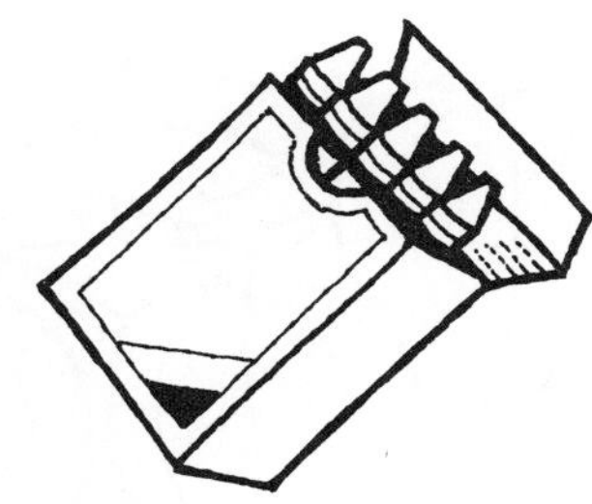 | 5 | 2 |
| 2. |  | | |
| 3. |   | | |
| 4. |  | | |
| 5. |  | | |

Write how many are inside and how many are outside.
Circle the number that is greater.

Name ____________________



# Less Than

Color orange the group of vegetables that has 1 less than the group of pumpkins.
Color red the group of vegetables that has 1 less than the group of peppers.
Color green the group of vegetables that has 1 less than the group of tomatoes.

Name ______________________________



# Order Through 10

Number the stepping stones in order.
Color the shortest path blue.
Color the longest path red.

Name ______________________________



# Ordinal Numbers

Start

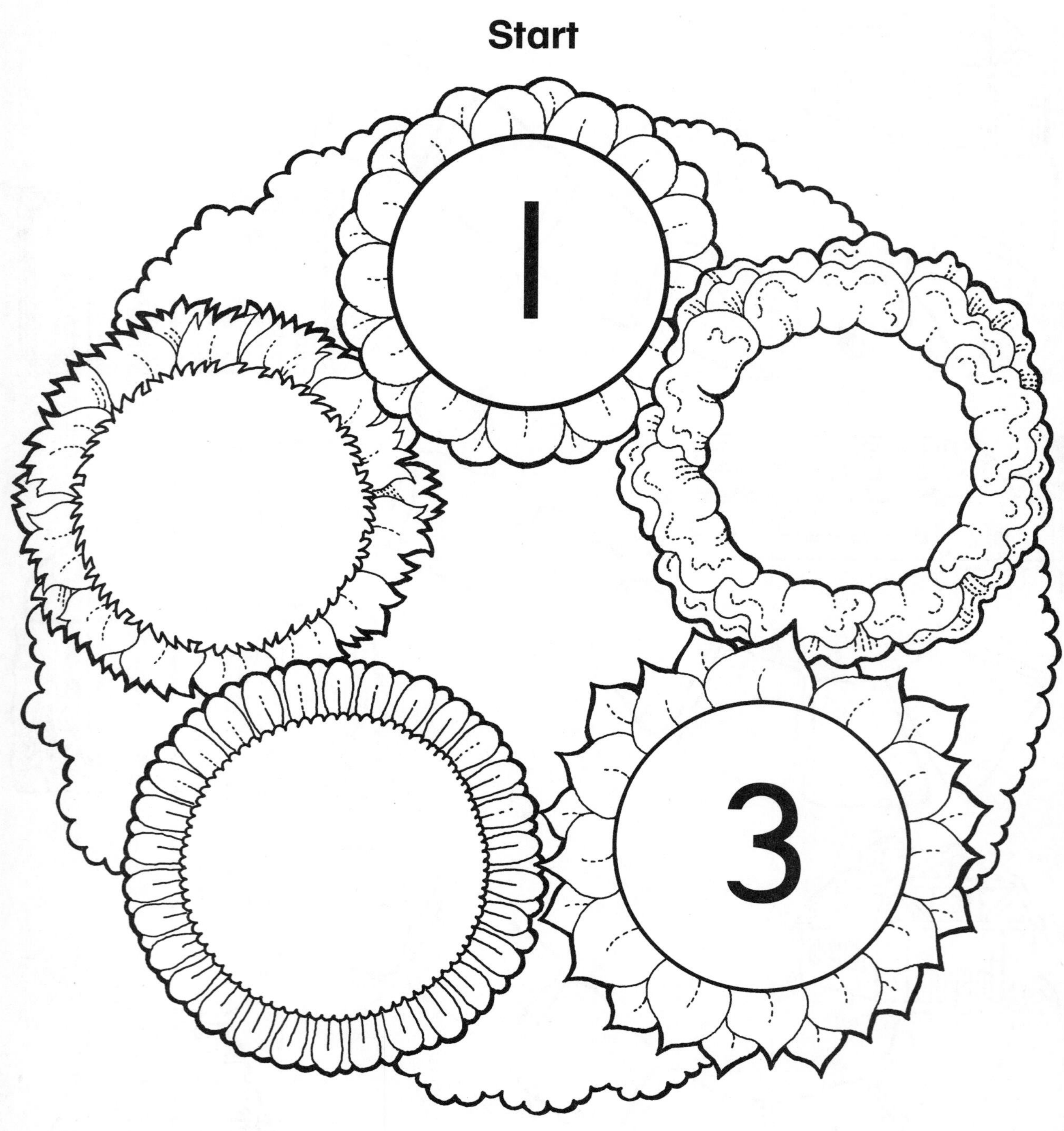


Go around the wreath. Color the second flower yellow.
Color the fourth flower red.
Color the fifth flower purple

Name ______________________________

# Modeling Addition Story Problems

Draw [flower] and [tulip].
Write how many in all.

1. Show one way to make 3.

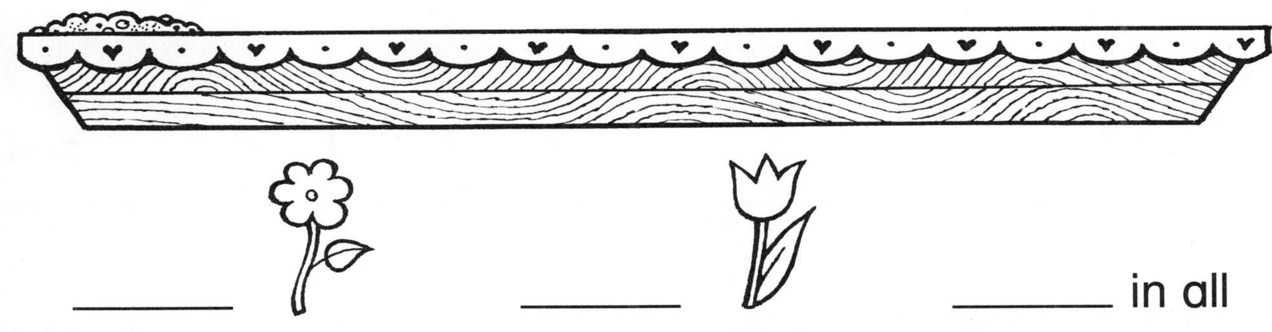

______ [flower] ______ [tulip] ______ in all

2. Show one way to make 6.

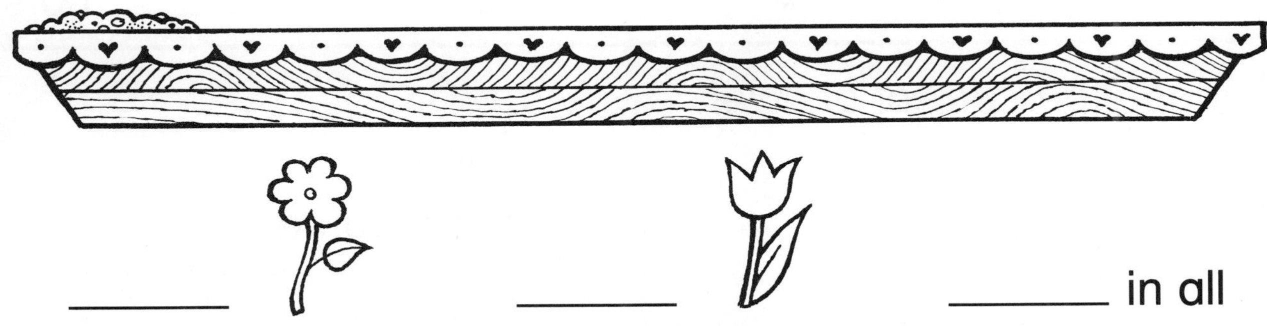

______ [flower] ______ [tulip] ______ in all

Make up an addition story.
How many in all? Mark your answer.

3.

1 ○ 2 ○ 3 ○

4.

4 ○ 5 ○ 6 ○

Name ____________________



# Adding 1

Draw 1 more.
Write the sum.

1. 1 fish.
   1 more comes.

1 + 1 = __2__ fish

---

2. 3 cats.
   1 more comes.

3 + 1 = ______ cats

---

Choose the correct answer.

3. 5 ducks.
   1 more comes.
   How many ducks?

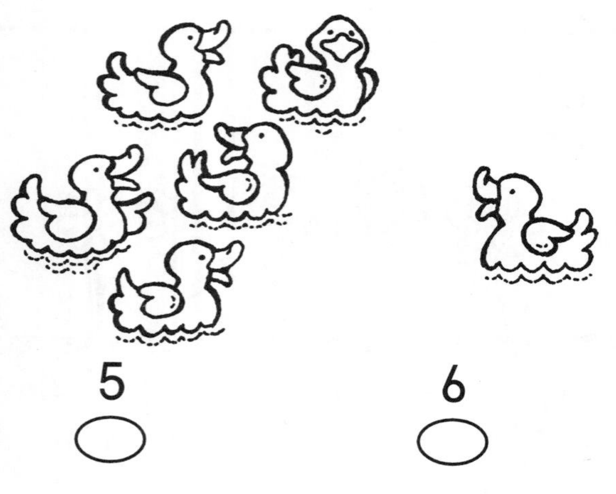

5 ◯  6 ◯

4. 4 sheep.
   1 more comes.
   How many sheep?

4 ◯  5 ◯

Name ______________________



# Adding 2

Draw 2 more.
Write the sum.

1. I cow.
   2 more come.

I + 2 = __3__ cows

2. 2 bears.
   2 more come.

2 + 2 = ____ bears

Choose the correct answer.

3. Which hat has 2 more than I?

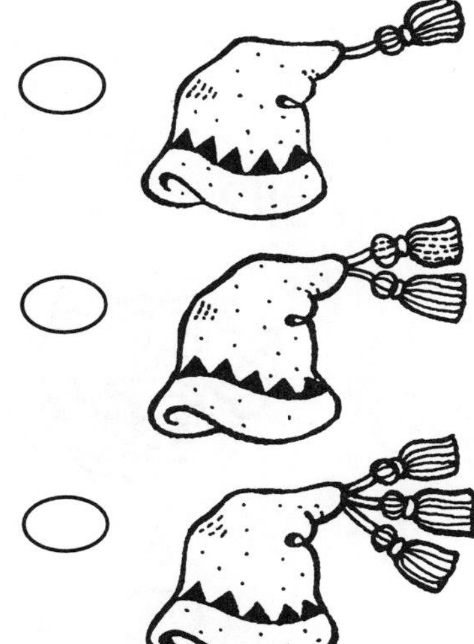

4. Which bunch has 2 more than 3?

Name ______________________



# Using Pictures to Add

Draw a picture.
Write the sum.

1. 2 birds sit.
3 birds eat.
How many in all?

2 + 3 = __5__ birds

2. 2 dogs run.
2 dogs jump.
How many in all?

2 + 2 = ____ dogs

3. 5 cows eat.
1 cow sleeps.
How many in all?

5 + 1 = ____ cows

Mark your answer.

4. 3 frogs hop.
3 frogs sit.
How many in all?

4 ○ 5 ○ 6 ○

5. 3 cats sit.
2 cats sleep.
How many in all?

4 ○ 5 ○ 6 ○

Name ____________________



# Reading Strategy • Use Pictures Clues

Using pictures can help you solve problems.

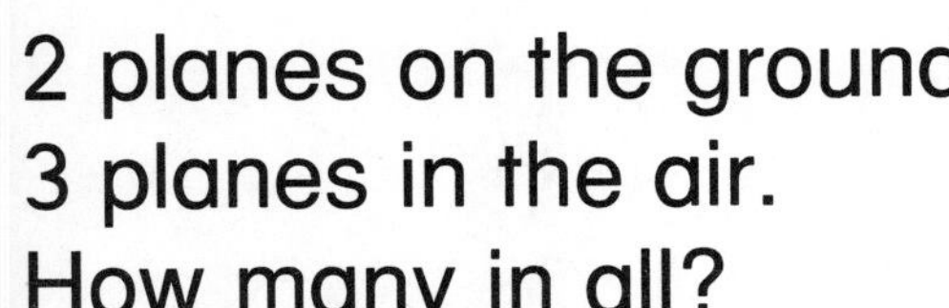

2 planes on the ground.
3 planes in the air.
How many in all?

Look at the picture.

1. Count the planes **on the ground.**

   2 planes

2. Count the planes **in the air.**

   ____ planes

3. Write the addition sentence.

   ___ + ___ = ___ planes

Solve.

4. 2 jets on the ground.
   2 jets in the air.
   How many in all?

___ + ___ = ___ jets

5. 3 planes on the ground.
   1 plane in the air.
   How many in all?

___ + ___ = ___ planes

Name ________________________________

LESSON 2.1

# Modeling Subtraction Story Problems

Make up a subtraction story problem.
Write how many.

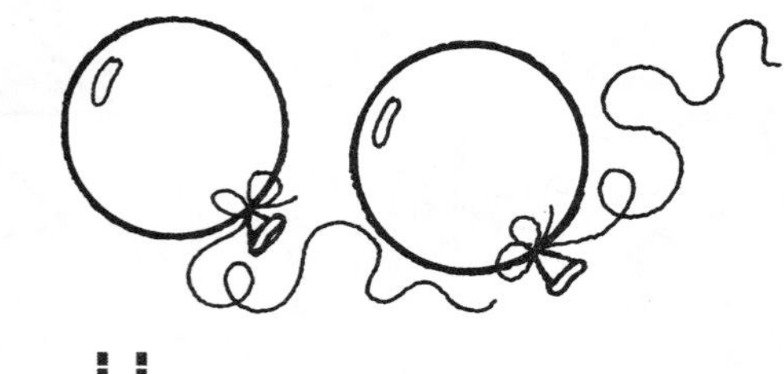

2 pop 2 are left

_____ snow people _____ melts _____ are left

_____ toy boats _____ sink _____ are left

Make up a subtraction story problem.
How many are left? Mark your answer.

4.

- ◯ 3
- ◯ 4
- ◯ 5
- ◯ 6

5.

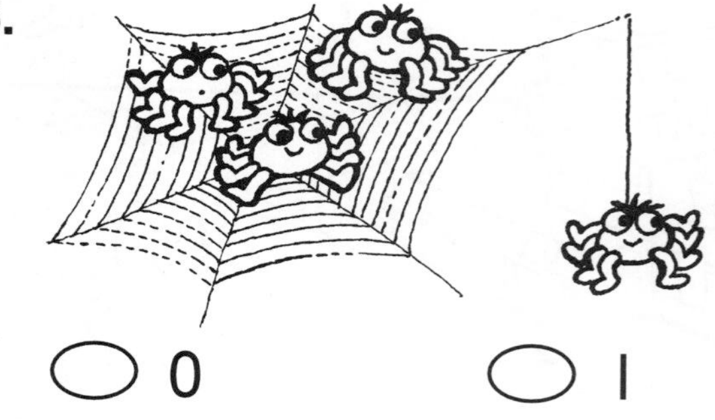

- ◯ 0
- ◯ 1
- ◯ 2
- ◯ 3

Name ______________________________

LESSON 2.2

# Subtracting 1

Cross out 1.
Write how many are left.

1. There are 4 apples.
   Jon eats 1.

How many are left? 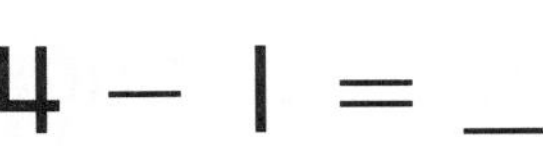 4 − 1 = __3__ apples

---

2. There are 6 pears.
   Nancy eats 1.

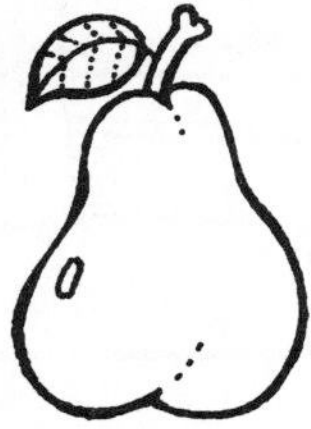     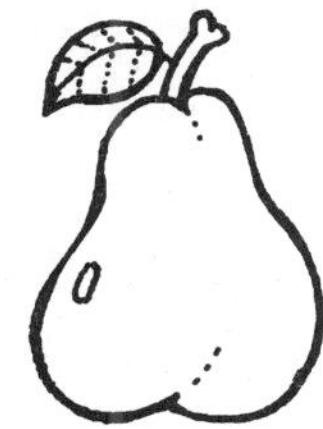

How many are left?  6 − 1 = _____ pears

---

3. There are 2 apples.
   Nat eats 1.
   How many are left?

  1 ◯ 2

 3 ◯ 4

4. There are 3 oranges.
   Angel eats 1.
   How many are left?

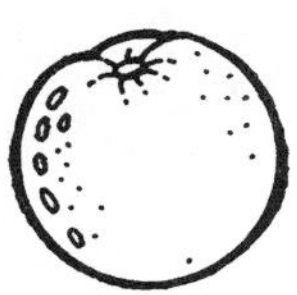  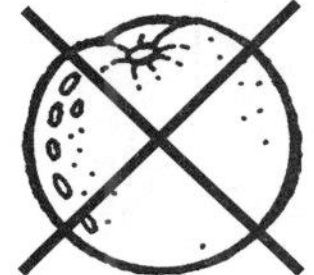

◯ 0  1

 2 ◯ 3

Name ______________________________

LESSON 2.3

# Subtracting 2

Cross out pictures to show the subtraction sentence. Write how many are left.

1. 4 bugs are on a leaf.
   2 fly away.
   How many are left?

$4 - 2 =$ __2__ bugs

2. 5 birds are on a fence.
   2 fly away.
   How many are left?

$5 - 2 =$ _____ birds

Choose the correct answer.

3. Which flag has 2 fewer than 6 stars?

4. Which animal has 2 fewer than 4 legs?

Name ____________________



# Writing Subtraction Sentences

Draw a picture.
Write the number sentence.

| | |
|---|---|
| 1. Pete has 5 balloons.<br>3 blow away.<br>How many are left?<br><br>5 − 3 = __2__ balloons | |
| 2. Kathy has 6 balloons.<br>She gives 3 away.<br>How many are left?<br><br>6 − 3 = _____ balloons | |
| 3. Mia has 4 balloons.<br>1 pops.<br>How many are left?<br><br>4 − 1 = _____ balloons | |

Which subtraction sentence tells how many are left?
Mark your answer.

4. 

- ◯ 5 − 4 = 1
- ◯ 5 − 3 = 2
- ◯ 5 − 2 = 3
- ◯ 5 − 1 = 4

5. 

- ◯ 4 − 0 = 4
- ◯ 4 − 1 = 3
- ◯ 4 − 3 = 1
- ◯ 4 − 4 = 0

Name ____________________



# Reading Strategy • Use Word Clues

Read the problem.
Look for word clues.
Solve the problem.

1. 4 dogs play.
   2 **run away**.
   How many are left?

There are __2__ dogs left.

2. 4 dogs play.
   2 **more** come.
   How many in all?

There are __6__ dogs in all.

Solve.

3. 6 kittens in a basket.
   3 get out.
   How many are left?

There are _____ kittens left.

4. 1 puppy sleeps.
   5 more come.
   How many in all?

There are _____ puppies in all.

Name ____________________

LESSON 3.1

# Order Property

Write a number sentence to solve each problem.

1. Lee has 2 green pens. She buys 1 red pen. How many pens does Lee have?

   2 + 1 = 3

2. Tim has 1 green pen. He buys 2 red pens. How many pens does Tim have?

   ____ + ____ = ____

3. Sal draws 1 red star. She draws 3 blue stars. How many stars does Sal draw?

   ____ + ____ = ____

4. Laura draws 3 red stars. She draws 1 blue star. How many stars does Laura draw?

   ____ + ____ = ____

Choose the two number sentences that show you can add in any order.

5. ◯ 3 + 1 = 4
   1 + 3 = 4

   ◯ 3 + 1 = 4
   2 + 2 = 4

   ◯ not here

6. ◯ 1 + 1 = 2
   2 + 2 = 4

   ◯ 2 + 4 = 6
   3 + 3 = 6

   ◯ 2 + 4 = 6
   4 + 2 = 6

Name ____________________



# Addition Combinations

Draw a picture.
Write the number sentence.

1. Jack sees 4 red birds.
   Jane sees 3 yellow birds.
   How many birds in all?

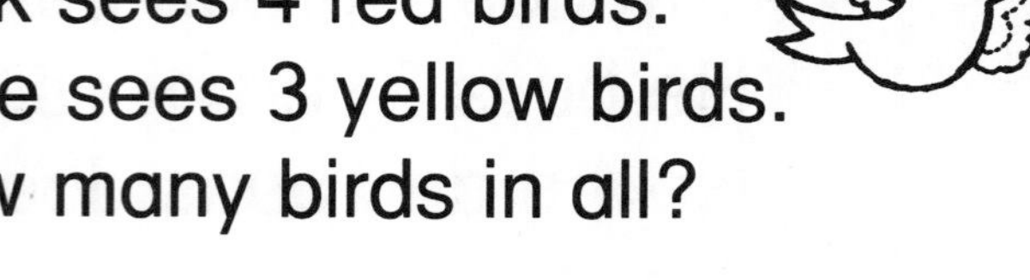
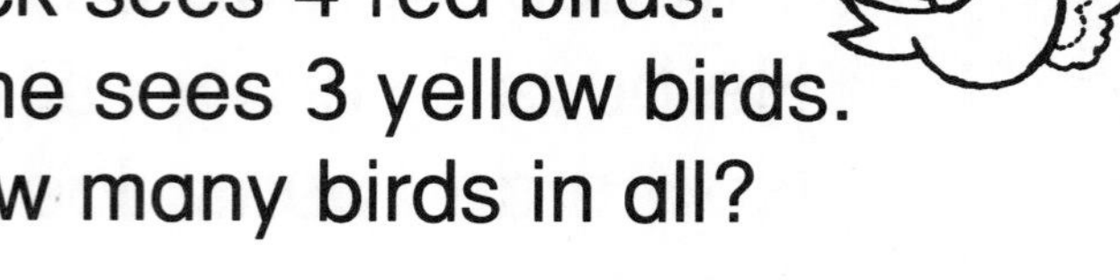

   4 + 3 = 7 birds

2. 3 birds eat seeds.
   5 more come.
   How many birds in all?

   ____ + ____ = ____ birds

3. 1 bird takes a bath.
   6 more come.
   How many birds in all?

   ____ + ____ = ____ birds

Mark the correct answer.

4. Which is a way to make 7?

   - ◯ 3 + 2
   - ◯ 2 + 4
   - ◯ 0 + 7
   - ◯ 1 + 7

5. Which is a way to make 8?
   - ◯ 4 + 4
   - ◯ 6 + 1
   - ◯ 2 + 4
   - ◯ 3 + 4

Name ____________________

LESSON 3.3

# More Addition Combinations

Draw a picture.
Write the number sentence.

1. Stan reads 4 books.
Tony reads 5 books.
How many books in all?

4 + 5 = 9 books

2. Mia checks out 2 books.
Zack checks out 6 books.
How many books in all?

____ + ____ = ____ books

3. 7 books are on the shelf.
2 books are on the desk.
How many books in all?

____ + ____ = ____ books

Mark the correct answer.

4. The sum of two numbers is 9. Which are the two numbers?

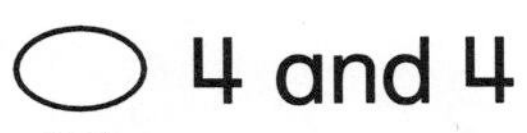

- ◯ 4 and 4
- ◯ 3 and 6
- ◯ 7 and 1
- ◯ 3 and 5

5. There are 10 children at a party. Which tells how many girls and boys there are?

- ◯ 3 girls and 3 boys
- ◯ 5 girls and 4 boys
- ◯ 3 girls and 6 boys
- ◯ 7 girls and 3 boys

Name ____________________



# Horizontal and Vertical Addition

Write the problem two ways.

1. Ned has 6 fish.
He buys 4 more.
How many fish in all?

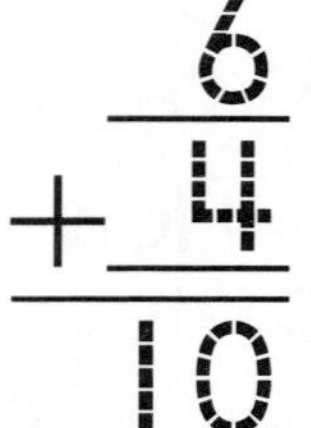

10 fish    6 + 4 = 10

$$\begin{array}{r} 6 \\ +\ 4 \\ \hline 10 \end{array}$$

2. Alice has 3 pennies.
She gets 6 more.
How many pennies in all?

_____ pennies    ___ + ___ = ___

$$\begin{array}{r} \_\_\_ \\ +\ \_\_\_ \\ \hline \_\_\_ \end{array}$$

Mark the correct answer.

3. Pam writes this addition sentence.

$3 + 5 = 8$

Which problem is the same?

- ○ $\begin{array}{r} 3 \\ +4 \\ \hline 7 \end{array}$
- ○ $\begin{array}{r} 3 \\ +5 \\ \hline 8 \end{array}$
- ○ $\begin{array}{r} 4 \\ +4 \\ \hline 8 \end{array}$

4. Ali writes this problem.

$$\begin{array}{r} 4 \\ +5 \\ \hline 9 \end{array}$$

Which addition sentence is the same?

- ○ $4 + 5 = 9$
- ○ $4 + 4 = 8$
- ○ $5 + 2 = 7$
- ○ $6 + 3 = 9$

Name ______________________________



# Reading Strategy • Using Pictures

Using pictures can help you solve problems.

Tammy buys a top.
She buys a doll.
How much does she spend?

1. Look at the pictures.
   Write the answer.
   How much does the top cost? __4__¢

   How much does the doll cost? ______¢

2. Write an addition sentence.
   Solve the problem.

   _____¢ + _____¢ = _____¢

Solve.

3. Jim buys a boat.
   He buys a car.
   How much does he spend?

____¢ + ____¢ = ____¢

4. Amy buys a ball.
   She buys jacks.
   How much does she spend?

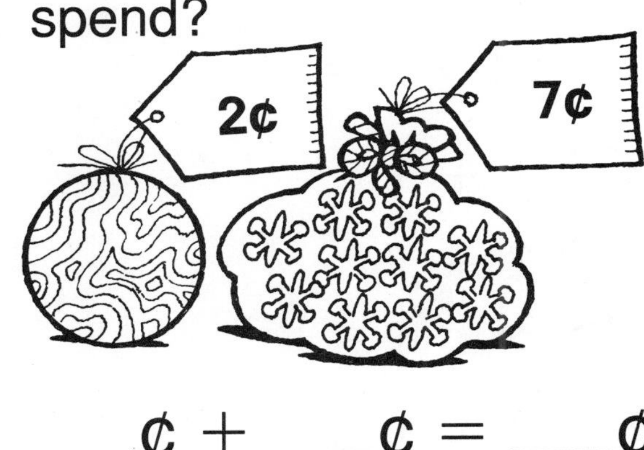


____¢ + ____¢ = ____¢

Name ______________________________



# Counting On 1 and 2

Count on to add.
Write the sum.

1. 

6 birds in a house.
1 more comes.
How many birds in all?

6 + 1 = 7 birds

2. 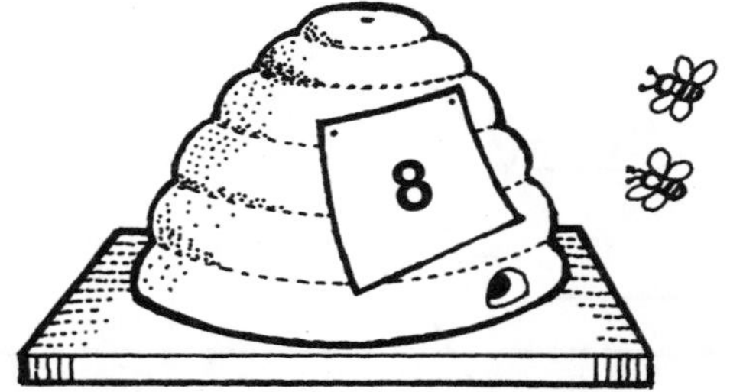


8 bees in a hive.
2 more come.
How many bees in all?

8 + 2 = _____ bees

3. 

3 bears in a cave.
2 more come.
How many bears in all?

3 + 2 = _____ bears

Mark the correct answer.

4. Which has same sum?

1 + 2 = _____

- ◯ 1 + 1
- ◯ 2 + 1
- ◯ 3 + 1
- ◯ 4 + 1

5. Which has same sum?

4 + 2 = _____

- ◯ 4 + 1
- ◯ 3 + 3
- ◯ 5 + 0
- ◯ 2 + 2

Name ____________________



# Counting On 3

Count on to add.
Write the sum.

1.

Jan has 4 pennies.
She gets 3 more.
How many pennies in all?

4 + 3 = 7 pennies

2.

Dave has 8 pennies.
He gets 2 more.
How many pennies in all?

8 + 2 = ____ pennies

3.

Rick 6 pennies.
He gets 3 more.
How many pennies in all?

6 + 3 = ____ pennies

Mark the correct answer.

4. Which is a way to make 4?

- ◯ 3 + 1
- ◯ 3 + 2
- ◯ 1 + 2
- ◯ 4 + 2

5. Which is a way to make 8?

- ◯ 5 + 1
- ◯ 5 + 3
- ◯ 5 + 2
- ◯ 5 + 4

Name ______________________________



# Doubles

Write a number sentence.

1. Annie has 5 crayons.
   Max has the same number.
   How many do they have in all?

   5 + 5 = 10 crayons

2. Jill has 4 pens.
   Nick has 4 more than Jill.
   How many does Nick have?

   ____ + ____ = ____ pens

Mark the correct answer.

3. Which doubles fact goes with the picture?

- ◯ 1 + 1 = 2
- ◯ 2 + 2 = 4
- ◯ 3 + 3 = 6
- ◯ 4 + 4 = 8

4. Which doubles fact goes with the picture?

- ◯ 2 + 2 = 4
- ◯ 3 + 3 = 6
- ◯ 4 + 4 = 8
- ◯ 5 + 5 = 10

Name ____________________



# Addition Facts Practice

Draw a picture.
Solve.

1. A bike has 2 wheels.
   A car has 4 wheels.
   How many wheels in all?

   6 wheels

2. A wagon has 4 wheels.
   How many wheels do
   2 wagons have?

   ______ wheels

3. A truck has 6 wheels.
   A van has 4 wheels.
   How many wheels in all?

   ______ wheels

Mark the correct answer.

4. Which is a doubles fact?

   ◯ $2 + 3 = 5$
   ◯ $2 + 2 = 4$
   ◯ $4 + 2 = 6$

5. Which is **not** a doubles fact?

   ◯ $4 + 3 = 7$
   ◯ $3 + 3 = 6$
   ◯ $4 + 4 = 8$

Name ______________________________



# Reading Strategy • Use Word Clues

Using word clues can help you solve problems.

Read the problem.
Look for word clues.
Draw a picture.
Solve.

1. Tom has **6 plants.**
He **gives 2 away**.
How many are left?

There are __4__ plants left.

2. **3 plants** are **big**.
**2 plants** are **little**.
How many plants in all?

______ plants

3. Toby has 2 big plants.
He buys 4 little plants.
How many plants in all?

______ plants

4. Mike picks 5 flowers.
He gives 3 away.
How many are left?

______ flowers

Name ______________________________

LESSON 5.1

# Subtraction Combinations

Draw a picture.
Subtract.

1. There are 8 carrots.
Beth eats 3.
How many carrots are left?

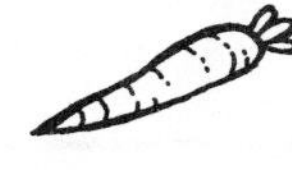

5 carrots

2. There are 7 plums.
Steve picks 4.
How many plums are left?

_____ plums

3. There are 8 beets.
Lynn eats 5.
How many beets are left?

_____ beets

Mark the correct answer.

4. Which subtraction sentence tells how many are left?

○ 6 − 3 = 3

○ 3 − 3 = 0

○ 4 − 3 = 1

○ 3 − 2 = 1

5. Which subtraction sentence tells how many are left?

○ 2 − 1 = 1

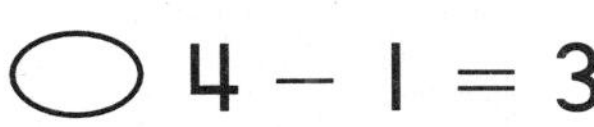
○ 4 − 1 = 3

○ 3 − 1 = 2

○ 4 − 4 = 0

Name ______________________________



# More Subtraction Combinations

Draw a picture.
Subtract.

1. Jean has 10 pennies.
   She spends 6.
   How many pennies are left?

4 pennies

2. Jim has 7 pennies.
   He spends 2.
   How many pennies are left?

_____ pennies

3. Nelda has 9 pennies.
   She spends 3.
   How many pennies are left?

_____ pennies

Mark the correct answer.

4. Which comes next?

$9 - 0 =$ _____
$9 - 1 =$ _____
$9 - 2 =$ _____

◯ $9 - 6 =$ _____
◯ $9 - 5 =$ _____
◯ $9 - 4 =$ _____
◯ $9 - 3 =$ _____

5. Which comes next?

$7 - 0 =$ _____
$7 - 1 =$ _____
$7 - 2 =$ _____

◯ $7 - 3 =$ _____
◯ $7 - 4 =$ _____
◯ $7 - 5 =$ _____
◯ $7 - 6 =$ _____

Name ______________________________

LESSON 5.3

# Vertical Subtraction

Write the problem two ways.

1. Ken sees 5 fish.
   He sees 2 swim away.
   How many are left?

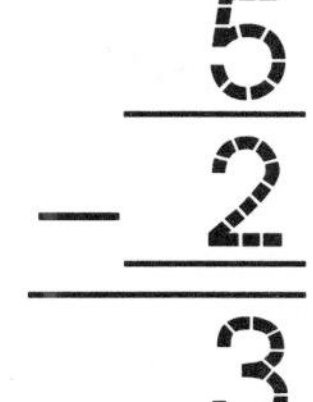

3 fish     5 − 2 = 3

---

2. Amy sees 10 butterflies.
   She sees 7 fly away.
   How many are left?

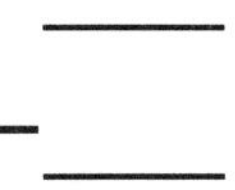

_____ butterflies     ___ − ___ = ___

---

Mark the correct answer.

3. Jody writes this subtraction sentence.

   7 − 3 = 4

   Which problem is the same?

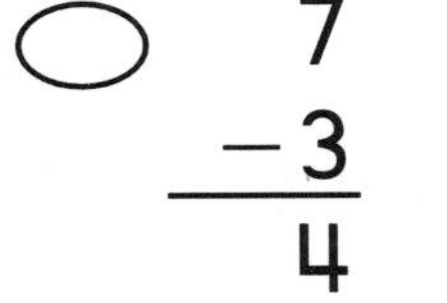

$$\begin{array}{r} 7 \\ -3 \\ \hline 4 \end{array}$$

◯
$$\begin{array}{r} 7 \\ -4 \\ \hline 3 \end{array}$$

4. Lou writes this problem.

$$\begin{array}{r} 7 \\ -2 \\ \hline 5 \end{array}$$

   Which subtraction sentence is the same?

   ◯ 7 − 2 = 5
   ◯ 7 − 0 = 7
   ◯ 7 − 5 = 2
   ◯ 5 − 2 = 5

Name ______________________________



# Fact Families

Write number sentences.

1. Mr. Hill gives Ann these numbers. What fact family can she write?

4 1 5

4 + 1 = 5

___ + ___ = ___

___ − ___ = ___

___ − ___ = ___

2. Mr. Hill gives Chris these numbers. What fact family can he write?

3 2 1

| 2 | ___ | ___ | ___ |
|---|---|---|---|
| + 1 | + ___ | − ___ | − ___ |
| 3 | ___ | ___ | ___ |

Mark the correct answer.

3. What are the numbers in this fact family?

4 + 4 = 8
8 − 4 = 4

○ 4, 8
○ 1, 4, 8
○ 0, 4, 8

4. What are the numbers in this fact family?

4 + 3 = 7
3 + 4 = 7
7 − 3 = 4
7 − 4 = 3

○ 4, 7, 11
○ 3, 4, 5
○ 4, 3, 7

Name ______________________________



# Subtracting to Compare

Draw a picture.
Subtract to compare.

1. Mia has 4 bowls.
   She has 2 fish.
   How many more bowls than fish does she have?

   __2__ more bowls

2. Rich has 5 dogs.
   He has 4 bones.
   How many more bones does he need?

   _____ more bone

Mark the correct answer.

3. Which number sentence goes with this picture?

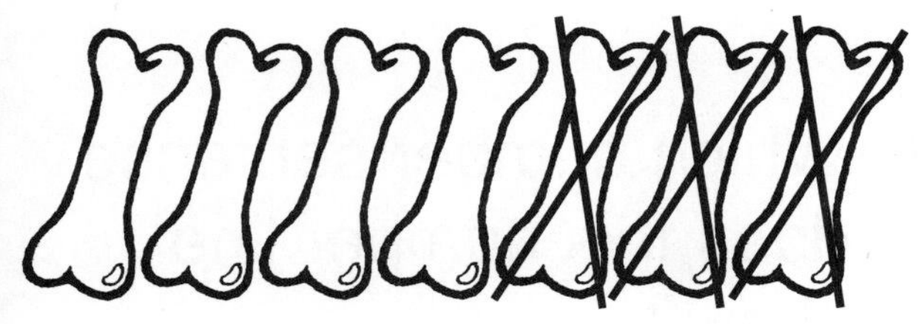

- ◯ $4 + 3 = 7$
- ◯ $3 + 4 = 7$
- ◯ $7 - 3 = 4$
- ◯ $7 - 7 = 0$

4. Which number sentence goes with this picture?

- ◯ $4 + 3 = 7$
- ◯ $3 + 4 = 7$
- ◯ $4 - 3 = 1$
- ◯ $7 - 3 = 4$

Name ______________________________

LESSON 6.1

# Counting Back 1 and 2

Use the number line.
Count back to subtract.

1. A robin is on number 8.
It takes 1 hop back.
What number is it on?

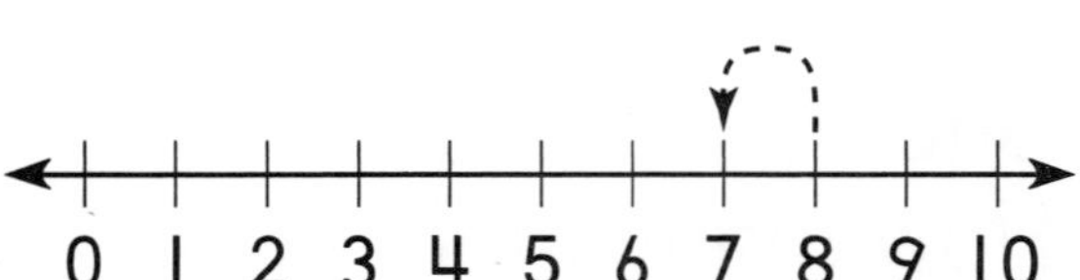


7

2. A bluebird is on number 10.
It takes 1 hop back.
What number is it on?

______

3. A crow is on number 7.
It takes 2 hops back.
What number is it on?

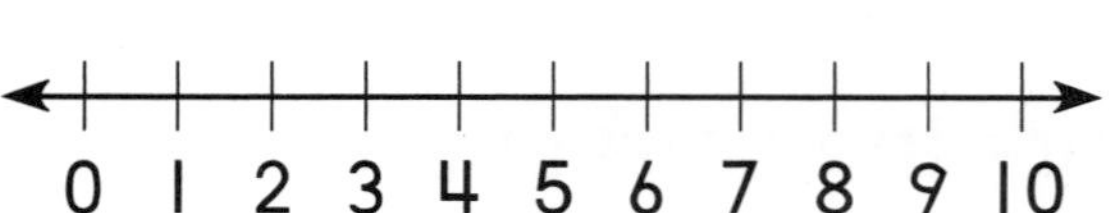


______

Mark the correct answer.

4. Which number sentence does this number line show?

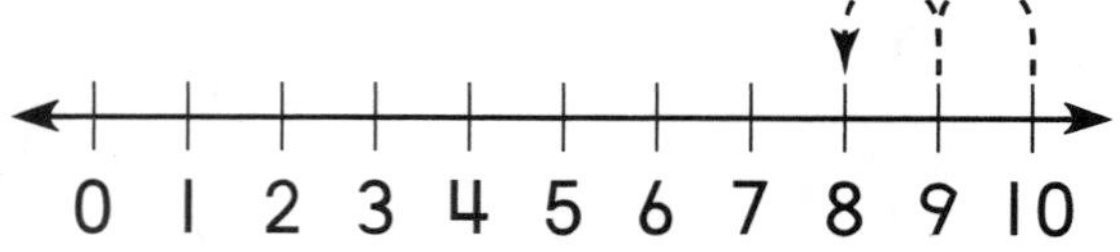


◯ $10 - 1 = 9$

◯ $10 - 2 = 8$

5. Which number sentence does this number line show?

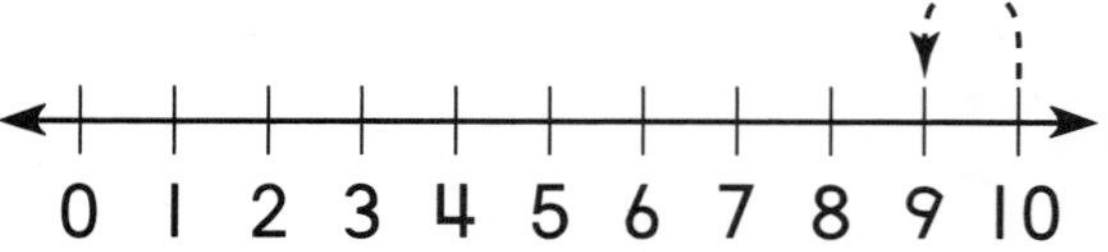


◯ $10 - 1 = 9$

◯ $10 - 3 = 7$

Name ____________________



# Counting Back 3

Use the number line.
Count back to subtract.

1. Fred stands on number 8.
He takes 3 hops back.
What number is he on now?

5

---

2. Megan stands on number 4.
She takes 2 hops back.
What number is she on now?

____

---

3. Winnie stands on number 6.
She takes 3 hops back.
What number is she on now?

____

---

Mark the correct answer.

4. Farley has 3 pennies.
He finds 1 more.
How many pennies does Farley have in all?

- ◯ 1 penny
- ◯ 2 pennies
- ◯ 4 pennies

5. Brooks has 3 pennies.
He loses 1 penny.
How many pennies does Brooks have left?

- ◯ 2 pennies
- ◯ 3 pennies
- ◯ 4 pennies

Name ______________________________



# Subtracting Zero

Draw a picture.
Write the subtraction sentence.

1. There are 4 crackers.
Ned eats 4.
How many are left?

4 – 4 = 0 crackers

2. There are 6 oranges.
Liza eats 0.
How many are left?

____ – ____ = ____ oranges

Mark the correct answer.

3. Which number sentence tells this story?

- ◯ 6 – 1 = 5
- ◯ 6 – 6 = 0
- ◯ 6 – 0 = 6
- ◯ not here

4. Which number sentence tells this story?

- ◯ 6 – 1 = 5
- ◯ 6 – 6 = 0
- ◯ 6 – 0 = 6
- ◯ not here

Name ____________________



# Facts Practice

Draw a picture.
Write the number sentence.

1. Carla has 7 leaves.
   She drops 3.
   How many leaves are left?

   7 – 3 = 4 leaves

2. Jim has 4 shells.
   He finds 2 more.
   How many shells in all?

   ____ + ____ = ____ shells

3. Pete has 8 nuts.
   He finds 1 more.
   How many nuts in all?

   ____ + ____ = ____ nuts

Mark the correct answer.

4. Which number names the sum?

   8 + 2 = ____

   ◯ 10
   ◯ 9
   ◯ 8

5. Which number names the difference?

   10 – 2 = ____

   ◯ 10
   ◯ 9
   ◯ 8

Name ______________________________

LESSON 6.5

# Reading Strategy • Use Word Clues and Pictures

Using word clues and pictures can help you solve problems.

Read the problem.
Look for word clues.
Look at the picture.
Cross out the frogs that hop away.
Solve.

1. 5 frogs sit on a log.
   2 **hop away**.
   How many now?

   5 − 2 = __3__ frogs

---

Solve.

2. 6 fish swim in a group.
   4 swim away.
   How many now?

______ fish

3. 3 crabs sit on the bottom.
   3 more come.
   How many now?

______ crabs

Name ______________________________



# Solid Figures

Color the toys.

1. Tina wants to play with spheres. Color them red.

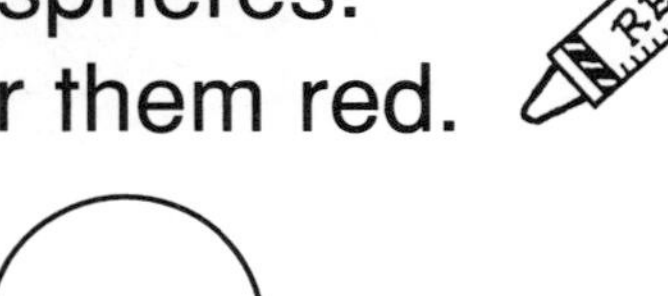

2. Matt wants to play with cones. Color them blue.

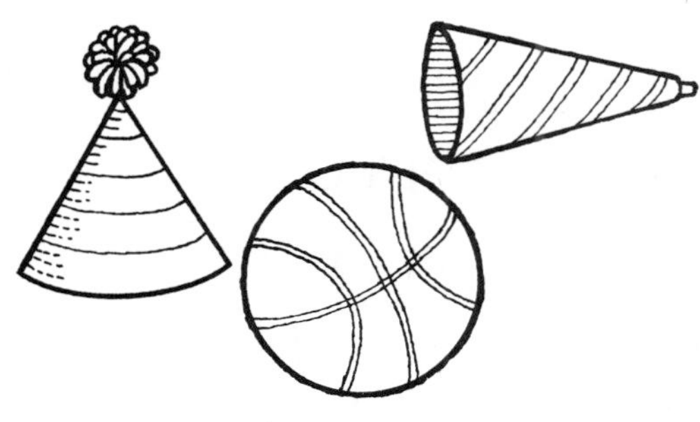

3. Luis wants to play with rectangular prisms. Color them yellow.

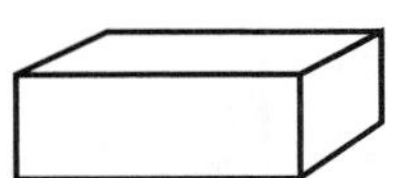

Which solid figure matches? Mark the answer.

4.

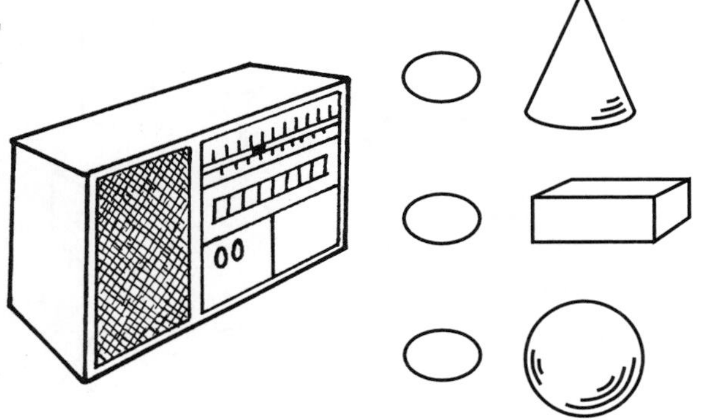

5.

Name ____________________



# More Solid Figures

Color the objects.

1. Look for things shaped like a pyramid. Color them brown.

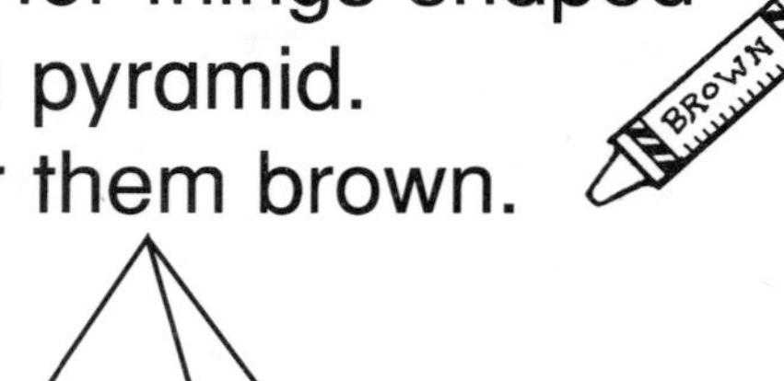

2. Look for things shaped like a cylinder. Color them green.

GREEN

3. Look for things shaped like a cube. Color them red.

RED

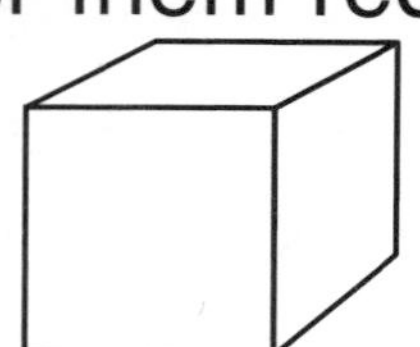

Which solid figure matches? Mark the answer.

4.

5.

Name ____________________



# Sorting Solid Figures

Circle the correct figures.

1. Ned wants to stack some blocks. Which blocks should he choose?

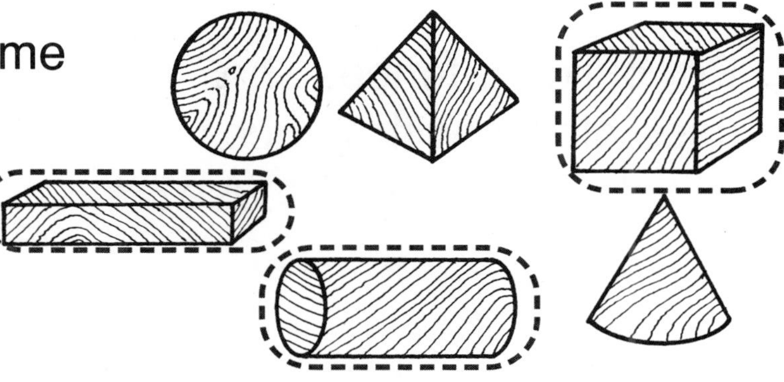

2. Jenny wants to slide blocks down a ramp. Which blocks should she choose?

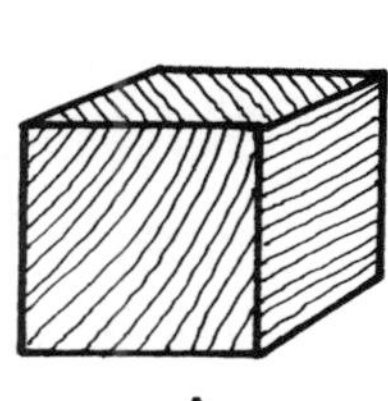

3. Tom wants to roll some toys down a ramp. Which toys should he choose?

4. Which figure will roll and stack?

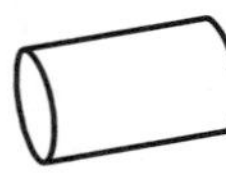
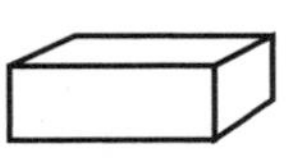

5. Which figure will slide but **not** roll?

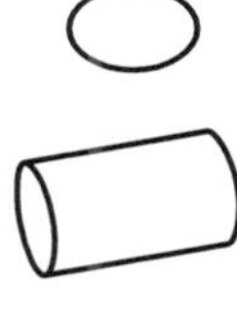

Name ____________________

LESSON 7.4

# More Sorting Solid Figures

Color the correct figures.

1. Pat builds a fence. She uses blocks with 2 faces. Which kind does she use?

2. Toby adds tops to some towers. He uses blocks with 1 face or 5 faces. Which kinds does he use?

3. Rita builds a house. She uses blocks that will slide and stack. Which kinds does she use?

Mark the correct answer.

4. How many faces?

 4

 5

 6

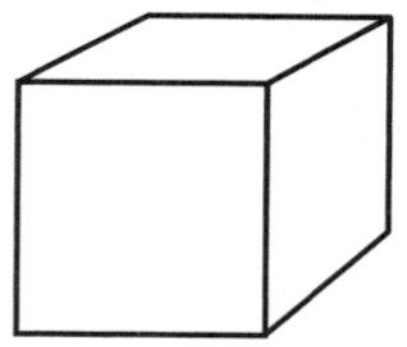

5. How many faces?

 0

 1

 2

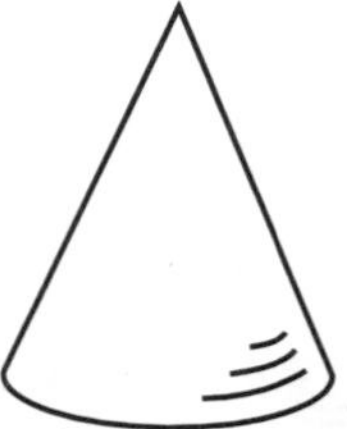

Name ____________________



# Reading Strategy • Use Picture Clues

Using picture clues can help you solve problems.

1. Look at the model.
   Count the cubes you see.

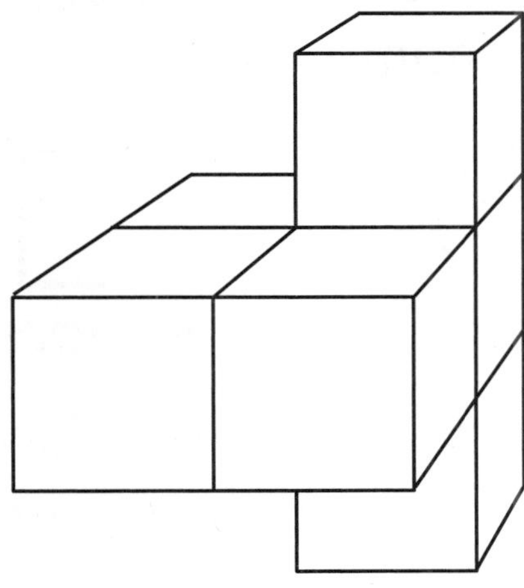

---

2. Look for hidden cubes.
   Count them.
   Write how many cubes.

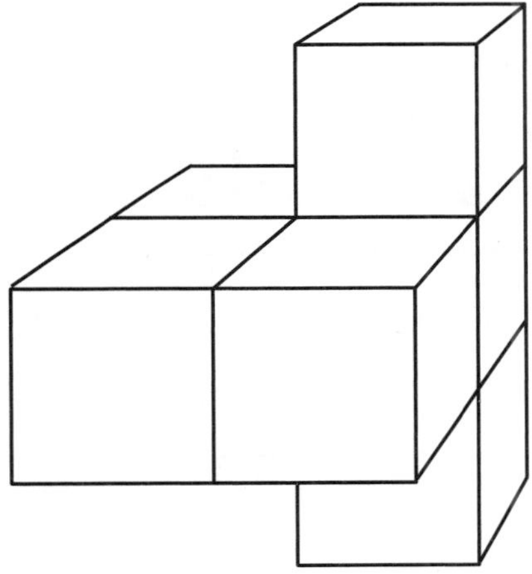

___6___ cubes

---

Write how many cubes.

3.

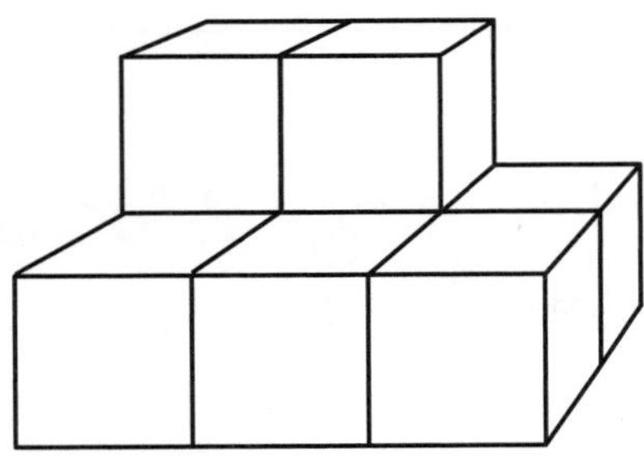

______ cubes

4.

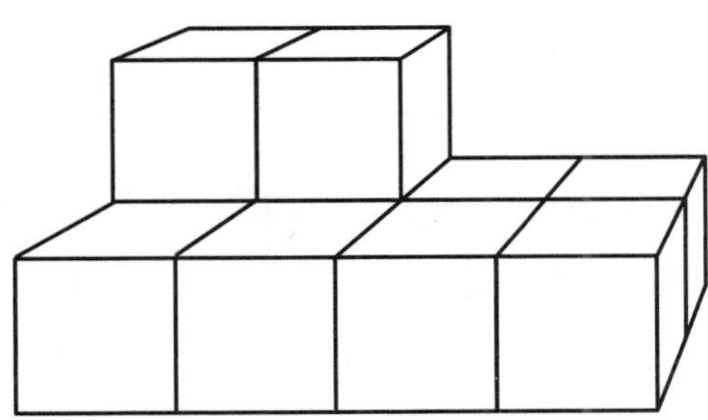

______ cubes

Name ______________________



# Plane Figures

Draw the correct shape.
Write its name.

circle

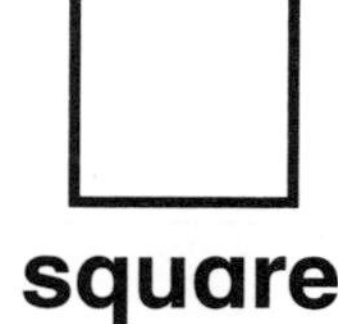
square

rectangle

triangle

1. Nan draws around a face.
What figure is the face?

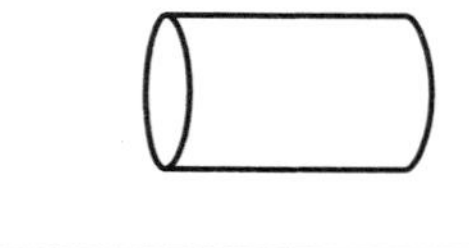

2. Tim draws around a face.
What figure is the face?

3. Nate draws around a face.
What figure is the face?

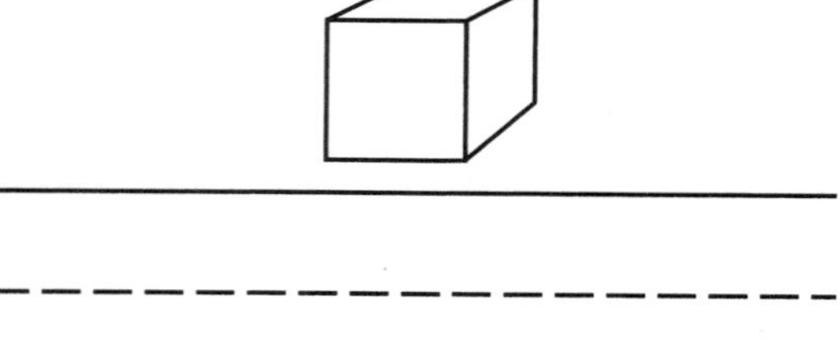

4. Pam draws around a face.
What figure is the face?

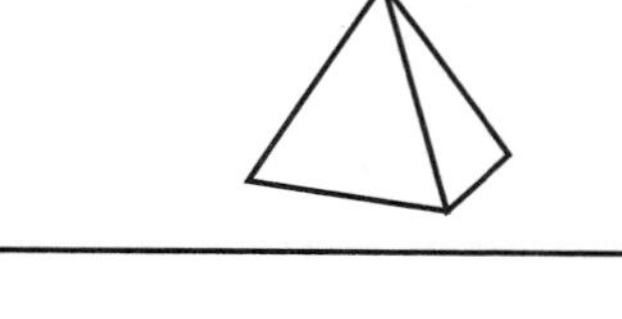

Mark the correct answer.

5. A cube has 6 faces shaped like me.
What am I?

○ square ○ rectangle
○ triangle ○ circle

6. A cylinder has 2 faces shaped like me.
What am I?

○ square ○ rectangle
○ triangle ○ circle

Name ____________________

LESSON 8.2

# Sorting Plane Figures

Draw the correct shape.

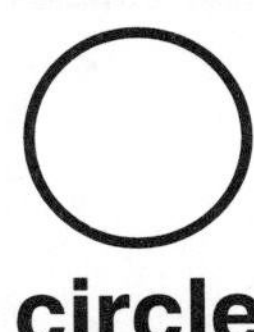
**circle**

**square**

**rectangle**

**triangle**

| | |
|---|---|
| 1. Patty chooses a shape with 0 sides and 0 corners. | |
| 2. Denny chooses a shape with 3 sides and 3 corners. | |
| 3. Renee chooses a shape that is a face on a cube. | |

Mark the correct answer.

4. Lee drew a closed figure with 6 sides. How many corners does it have?

   ◯ 4 corners

   ◯ 6 corners

   ◯ 8 corners

5. Don drew a closed figure with 4 sides and 4 corners. Which figure did he draw?

   ◯ square

   ◯ circle

   ◯ triangle

Name ________________________________



# Congruence

Draw a figure.

1. Karen makes a toy cat. She draws this pattern for the cat's ears. Draw a figure that is the same size and shape.

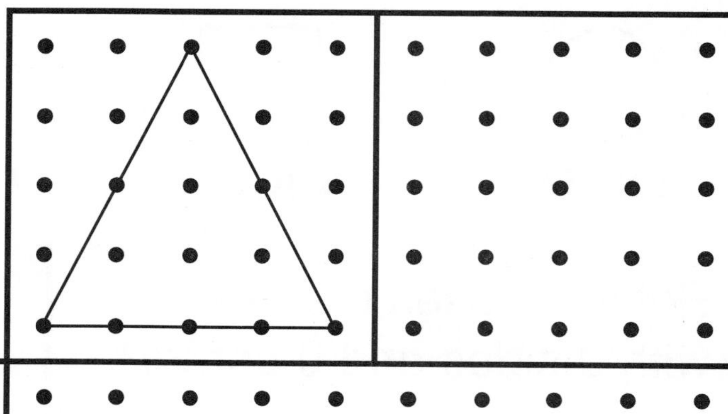

2. Ben makes a clown puppet. He traces around a cube for the buttons. Show what he draws.

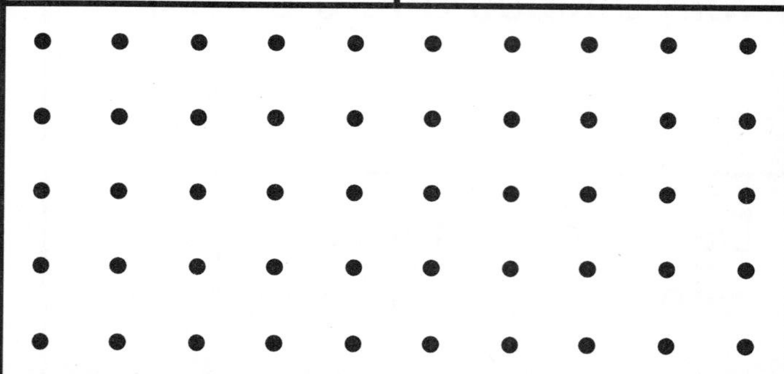

3. These figures are _____.

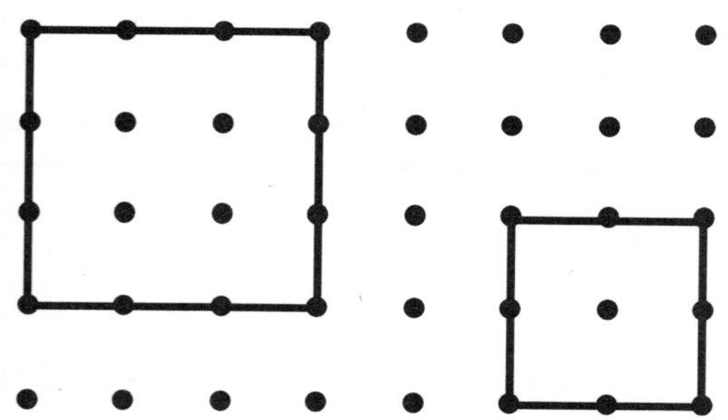

○ the same size

○ the same shape

○ the same size and shape

4. Which objects have the same size and shape?

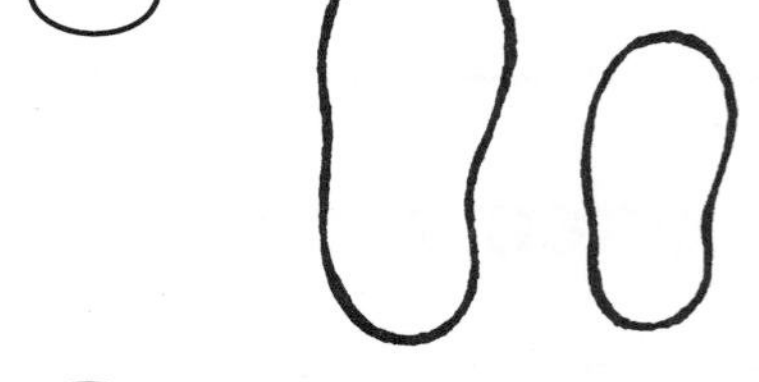

Name ______________________________



# Symmetry

Solve.

1. Ruth wants leaves that have 2 sides that match. Draw lines to show the ones she should keep.

2. Dave looks for shells that have the same size and shape. Color the ones he should keep.

3. Polly looks for flowers that have 2 sides that match. Draw lines to show the ones she should keep.

4. Steve looks for stamps that have 3 corners and 3 sides. Color the ones he should keep.

Mark the correct answer.

5. How many ways can you divide this kite into two sides that match?

- ◯ 1 way
- ◯ 2 ways
- ◯ 3 ways

6. On which word can you draw a line to make two sides that match?

- ◯ WOW
- ◯ WILL
- ◯ WON

Name ______________________________



# Open and Closed

Draw the figure.
Write **open** or **closed.**

1. Tony draws a figure.
   It has 4 sides and 3 corners.

   This figure is open.

2. Nick draws a figure.
   It has 7 sides and 7 corners.

   This figure is ______________.

3. Sally draws a figure.
   It has 6 sides and 5 corners.

   This figure is ______________.

Mark the correct answer.

4. Which name begins with a closed letter?
   - ○ Carol
   - ○ Bob
   - ○ Mary
   - ○ Saul

5. Which name begins with an open letter?
   - ○ Jack
   - ○ Doug
   - ○ Oliver
   - ○ Bill

Name ____________________



# Inside, Outside, On

Draw a picture.
Solve.

1. Tom draws a nest.
He draws 2 birds **inside** the nest.
He draws 1 bird **on** the nest.
He draws 2 birds **outside** the nest. How many birds in all?

5 birds

2. Simon draws a rectangle.
He draws a circle **inside** the rectangle.
He draws a square that is **outside** the circle but **inside** the rectangle.
Show what Simon draws.

Mark the correct answer.

3. Where is the man?

- ◯ inside the car
- ◯ on the car
- ◯ outside the car

4. Where is the bird?

- ◯ inside the birdhouse
- ◯ on the birdhouse
- ◯ outside the birdhouse

Name ______________________________



# Reading Strategy • Use Word Clues

Use the position words **left** and **right** to find where the friends will meet.

1. Find the X.
2. Walk right until you see the bench.
3. Turn and walk to the right of the slide.
4. Turn left at the tree.
5. Walk until you see me.

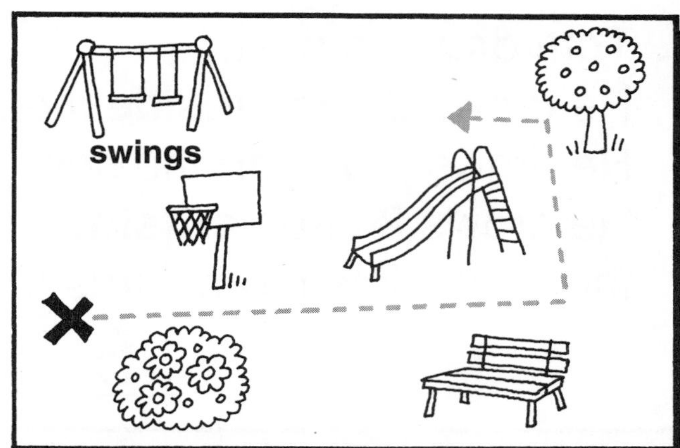


**left** **right**

1. Read all the directions. Look for the position words **left** and **right**.

2. Follow each direction. Use the position words. Mark the path you would take.

3. Solve the problem. Where will the friends meet?

______________________________

Solve.

4. Draw a picture of your playground. Draw yourself to the **right** of your favorite place to play.

Name ________________________________________

LESSON 9.4

# Positions on a Grid

Draw pictures on the grid.

Start at the ☆.

↑ Up

Right →

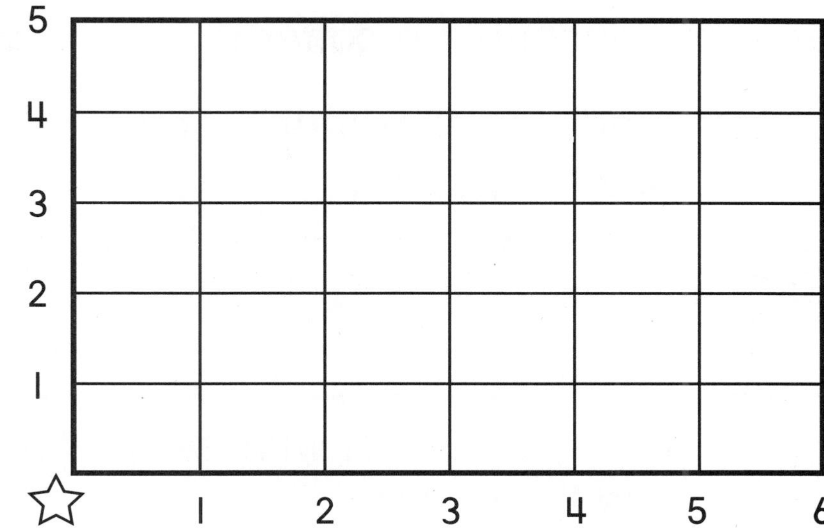


1. Lin lives in a house 3 spaces to the right and 3 spaces up.

   Draw a .

2. A tree grows 1 space to the right and 2 spaces up. Draw a  .

3. Lin likes to fish in a pond. It is 4 spaces to the right and 4 spaces up.

   Draw a .

4. Lin helps her dad shop at a store. It is 5 spaces to the right and 1 space up.

   Draw a .

Use the grid.
Mark the correct answer.

5. Which is to the left of Lin's house?

   ◯ 

   ◯ 

   ◯ 

6. Which is farthest to the right?

   ◯ 

   ◯ 

   ◯ 

Name ____________________



# Identifying Patterns

Draw to continue the pattern.

1. Beth made a belt with this pattern. Continue the pattern.

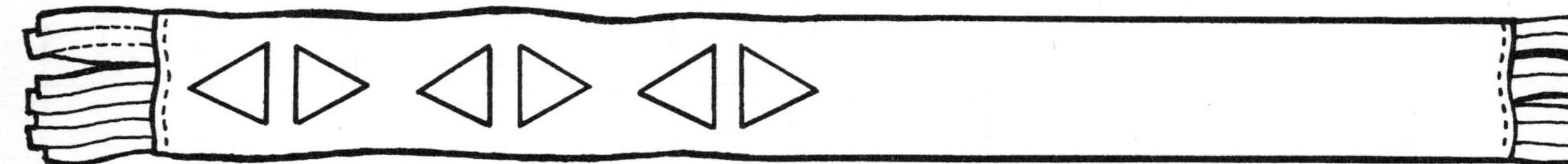

2. Ken made a bracelet with this pattern. Continue the pattern.

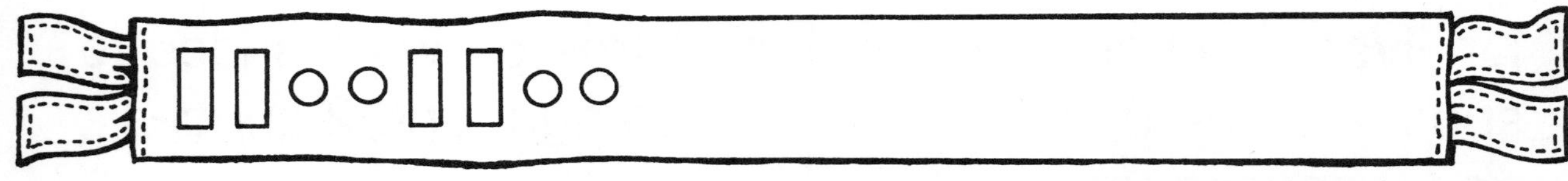

3. Saul made a belt with this pattern. Continue the pattern.

Mark the correct answer.

4. What is next in this pattern?

- ○
- □

5. What is the rule for this pattern?

- triangle, circle
- square, circle, triangle
- triangle, circle, square

Name ______________________________

LESSON 10.2

# Reproducing and Extending Patterns

Draw and color these patterns.

1. Marie uses red blocks to make the pattern triangle, square, circle. Draw her pattern two times.

---

2. Tom uses cubes to make the pattern yellow, red, red. Draw his pattern two times.

---

3. Jeff uses red squares and blue circles to make the pattern square, circle, circle. Draw his pattern two times.

---

Mark the correct answer.

4. What shape comes next?

5. Which shows the pattern square, triangle?

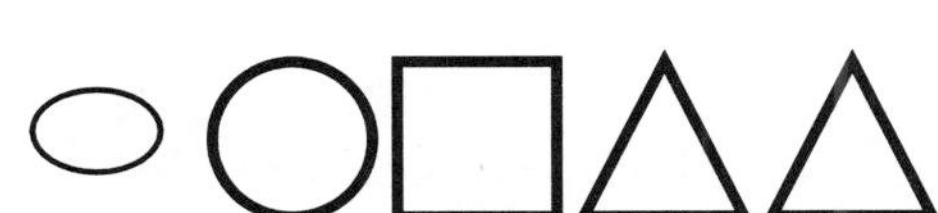

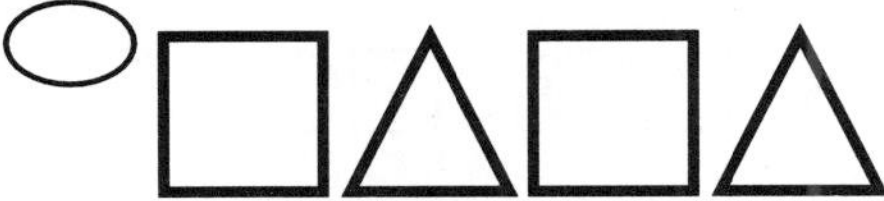

Name ________________________________



# Making and Extending Patterns

Draw and color these patterns.

1. Glenn has 3 circles, 3 squares, and 3 triangles. Show a pattern he can make.

2. Arlene has 3 circles and 6 cubes. Show a pattern she can make.

3. Carol uses green circles, red squares, and blue triangles to make the pattern square, triangle, circle. Draw her pattern three times.

Mark the correct answer.

4. Find a different pattern that uses the same shapes as this one.

5. Which shapes come next in the pattern?

Name ______________________

LESSON 10.4

# Reading Strategy • Make Predictions

Making predictions can help you solve problems.

Ruth makes this pattern with beads.
There is a mistake in the pattern.
What mistake do you see?

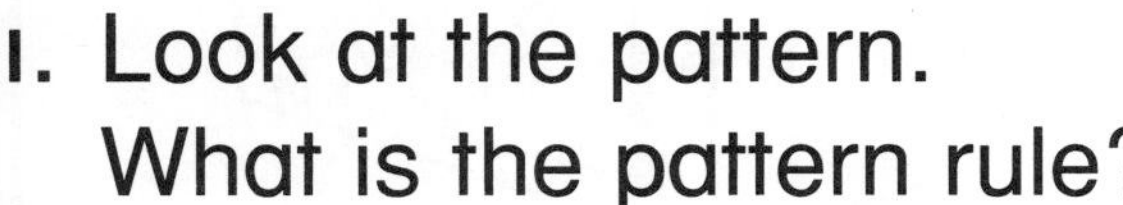

1. Look at the pattern.
   What is the pattern rule?

   square, triangle, triangle

2. Use the pattern rule.
   Say the first 7 shapes
   in Ruth's pattern.

3. Make a prediction.
   What comes next in the pattern?
   Circle the mistake.
   Draw the correct pattern.

Find the pattern rule. Circle the mistake.
Make a prediction and continue the pattern.

4. Tim makes this block pattern. Circle the mistake. Draw the correct pattern.

5. Nora makes this bead pattern. Circle the mistake. Draw the correct pattern.

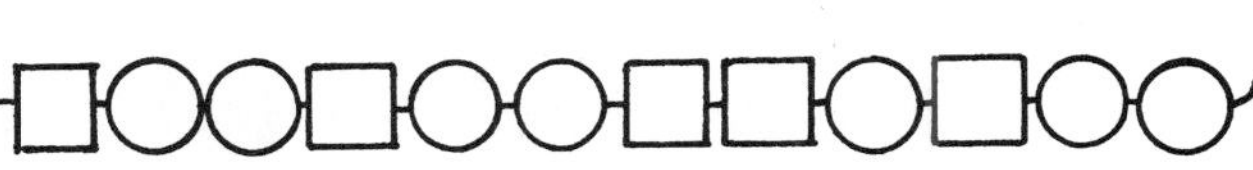

Name ____________________



# Counting On to 12

Draw how many come.
Write the sum.

1. 8 children are in the playhouse. 2 more come. How many children in all?

8 + 2 = 10

2. 8 children are in the sub. 3 more come. How many children in all?

____ + ____ = ____

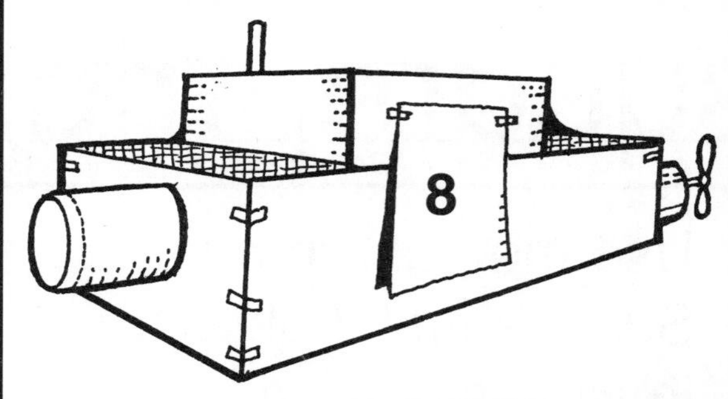


3. 9 children make a snow fort. 3 more come. How many children in all?

____ + ____ = ____

Mark the correct answer.

4. Count on. Which number is the sum?

9 + 2 = ____

- ◯ 11
- ◯ 13
- ◯ 12
- ◯ 14

5. Count on. Which numbers have the sum 11?

- ◯ 3 + 9
- ◯ 9 + 2
- ◯ 8 + 2
- ◯ 2 + 3

Name ______________________________



# Doubles to 12

Draw a picture.
Write the doubles facts.

1. Mrs. Green buys 2 baskets of apples. How many apples does she buy?

   5 + 5 = 10 apples

2. Mr. Wills buys 2 baskets of pineapples. How many pineapples does he buy?

   ____ + ____ = ____ pineapples

3. Ms. Young buys 2 baskets of plums. How many plums does she buy?

   ____ + ____ = ____ plums

Mark the correct answer.

4. Which is a doubles fact?

   ◯ 6 + 4 = 10
   ◯ 6 + 5 = 11
   ◯ 6 + 6 = 12
   ◯ not here

5. Which is not a doubles fact?

   ◯ 3 + 3 = 6
   ◯ 4 + 4 = 8
   ◯ 5 + 5 = 10
   ◯ 6 + 5 = 11

Name ______________________________



# Three Addends

Use [cube]. Draw them.
Write the sum.

1. Ben scores 2 points.
Marge scores 5 points.
Lynn scores 5 points.
How many points in all?

12 points

2. Paul hits 4 runs.
Mary hits the same number.
How many runs in all?

______ runs

Mark the correct answer.

3. Which team scored more points?

| Lions | Tigers |
|---|---|
| 2 | 1 |
| 3 | 4 |
| 4 | 3 |

◯ Tigers
◯ Lions

4. Which sum is the same as 3 + 2 + 5?

◯ 5 + 2 + 2
◯ 3 + 3 + 2
◯ 8 + 0 + 2
◯ 4 + 1 + 2

Name ____________________



# Practice the Facts

Draw a picture.
Write the number sentence.

1. Carl spends 7¢.
   Jill spends 1¢.
   Bob spends 4¢.
   How much do they spend?
   7 + 1 + 4 = 12¢

2. A pencil costs 8¢.
   A pen costs 2¢ more.
   How much does a pen cost?
   ____ + ____ = ____¢

3. Pete spends 4¢.
   Bill spends the same amount.
   How much do they spend?
   ____ + ____ = ____¢

Mark the correct answer.

4. Which prices have a sum of 10¢?

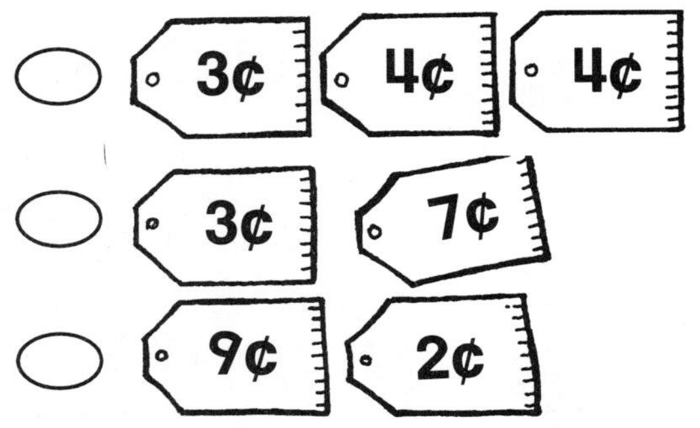


5. Lois has 10¢. Which toy could she buy?

Name ____________________



# Reading Strategy • Use Word Clues

Sometimes problems use repeated words. Using **word clues** can help you read and solve problems.

**8 fish** hide.
**2 more fish** hide.
How many fish hide?

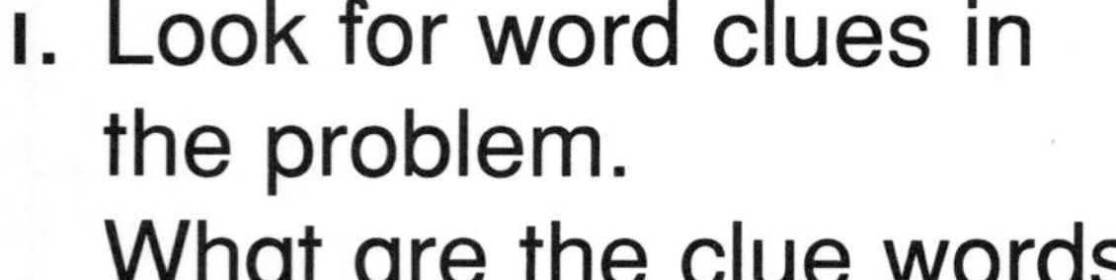

1. Look for word clues in the problem. What are the clue words? ____________________

2. Draw a picture. Write an addition sentence to solve the problem.

   ___ + ___ = ___

   ___ fish

Solve.

3. 7 frogs sit on a rock. 4 more frogs sit. How many frogs sit?

   ___ + ___ = ___

   ___ frogs

Name ____________________

LESSON 12.1

# Relating Addition and Subtraction

Write a number sentence.
Solve.

| | |
|---|---|
| 1. Nora has 5 apples. She picks 2 more. How many apples does she have in all? | 5 (+) 2 = 7 apples |
| 2. Nora has 7 apples. She eats 2. How many apples does she have left? | ___ (−) ___ = ___ apples |
| 3. Bob has 9 plums. He eats 1. How many plums does he have left? | ___ (−) ___ = ___ plums |

Mark the correct answer.

4. The sum of two numbers is 9. One number is 6. What is the other number?

- ◯ 2
- ◯ 3
- ◯ 4
- ◯ not here

5. The sum of two numbers is 12. One number is 5. What is the other number?

- ◯ 7
- ◯ 6
- ◯ 5
- ◯ not here

Name ______________________



# Counting Back

Count back or count on to solve.

1. Betty stands on number 6. She takes 2 hops back. What number is she on now? 4

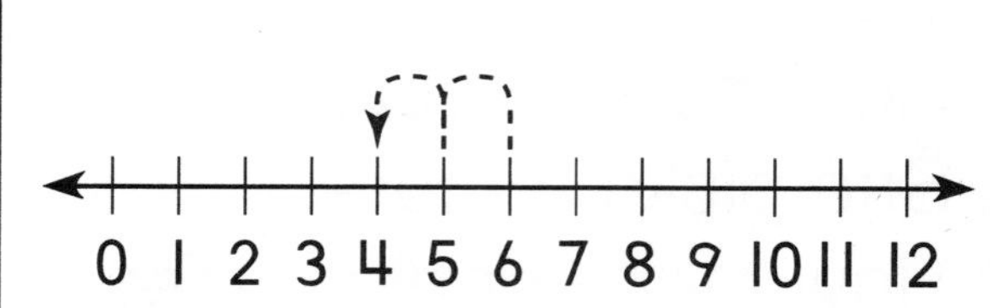


2. Ann stands on number 8. She takes 3 hops forward. What number is she on now? ____

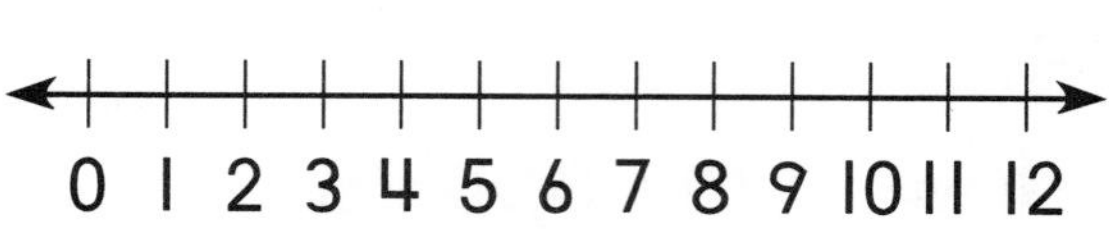


3. Stan stands on number 11. He takes 3 hops back. What number is he on now? ____

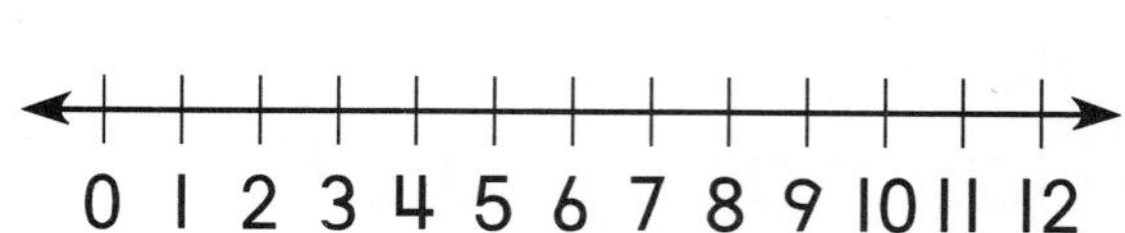


Mark the correct answer.

4. Count back. Which is the difference?

$9 - 2 =$ ____

- ◯ 7
- ◯ 8
- ◯ 9
- ◯ 10

5. Count on. Which is the sum?

$9 + 2 =$ ____

- ◯ 10
- ◯ 11
- ◯ 12
- ◯ 13

Name ______________________________



# Compare to Subtract

Draw a picture.
Solve.

1. There are 12 children in line. The bus has 8 seats. How many fewer seats than children are there?

   4 fewer seats

2. There are 9 people waiting for the bus. The bus has 7 empty seats. How many more people than seats are there?

   _____ more people

Mark the correct answer.

3. Which question goes with the problem?
   There are 8 children.
   4 children leave.
   - ◯ How many children in all?
   - ◯ How many children are left?
   - ◯ How many more children are there?

4. Which question goes with the problem?
   There are 9 children.
   3 more children come.
   - ◯ How many children in all?
   - ◯ How many children are left?
   - ◯ How many fewer children are there?

Name ______________________________



# Fact Families

Draw a picture.
Write the number sentence.

| | |
|---|---|
| 1. Martha has 5 red blocks. She has 3 blue blocks. How many blocks does Martha have? | 5 (+) 3 = 8 blocks |
| 2. Toby has 8 cars. He gives 3 cars to his sister. How many cars does Toby have left? | ___ (−) ___ = ___ cars |
| 3. Jan lines up 6 number cards. She counts back 3 cards from 6. On what number does she stop? ___ | |

Mark the correct answer.

4. Which number sentence belongs in this fact family?

   8 + 3 = 11

   - ◯ 8 + 4 = 12
   - ◯ 8 + 2 = 10
   - ◯ 11 − 4 = 7
   - ◯ 11 − 3 = 8

5. Which number sentence belongs in this fact family?

   5 + 5 = 10

   - ◯ 10 − 0 = 10
   - ◯ 10 − 5 = 5
   - ◯ 6 + 6 = 12
   - ◯ 6 + 4 = 10

Name ____________________

LESSON 12.5

# Reading Strategy • Reread

Rob has 8 forks.
He has 12 plates.
How many fewer forks than plates does Rob have?

1. Read the problem.
Write a number sentence.

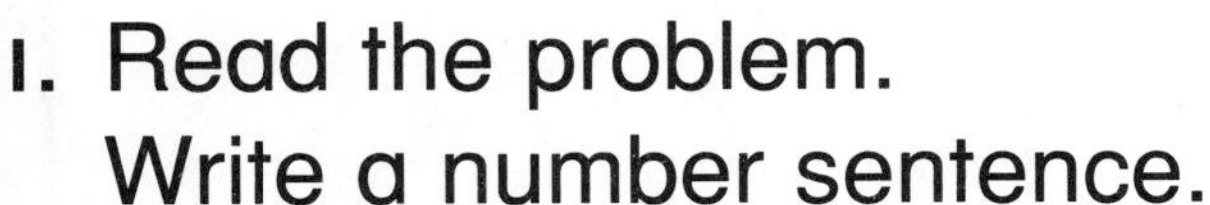

$12 - 8 =$ ____

---

2. Reread the problem.
Make sure the numbers you wrote match the numbers in the problem.
8 forks
12 plates

---

3. Look for words that tell you what to do.
The words **how many fewer** tell you to compare two groups and subtract.

---

4. Solve the problem.
$12 - 8 =$ ____ fewer forks

---

Solve.

5. Rob has 11 straws.
He has 9 cups.
How many more straws than cups are there?

____ more straws

6. Rob has 12 bows.
He has 7 balloons.
How many fewer balloons than bows are there?

____ fewer balloons

Name ______________________



# Tens

Draw a picture.
Write how many groups of ten.

1. Paul has 40 apples. How many bags of 10 apples can he make?

   4 bags of 10

2. Nick has 60 pears. How many bags of 10 pears can he make?

   ______ bags of 10

3. Rosa has 80 nuts. How many bags of 10 nuts can she make?

   ______ bags of 10

How many counters?
Mark the correct answer.

4. 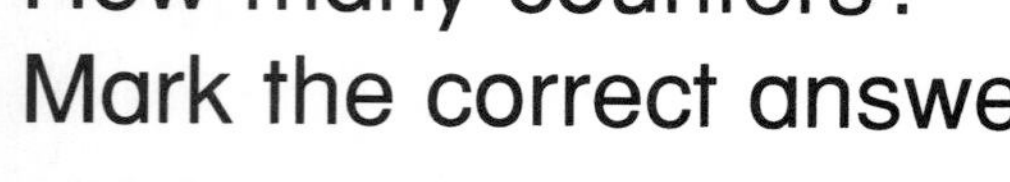
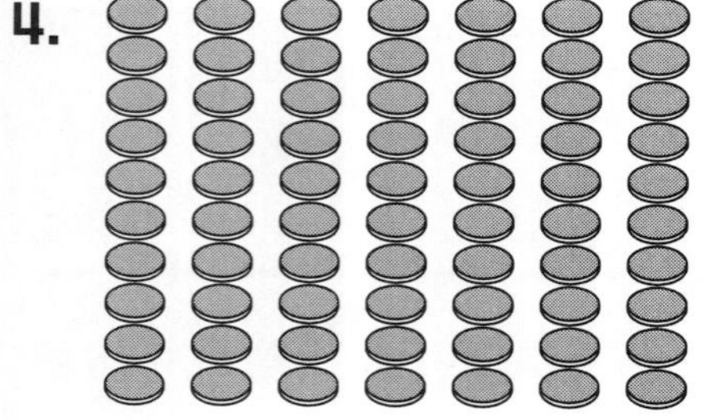

- ◯ 5 tens = 50
- ◯ 6 tens = 60
- ◯ 7 tens = 70
- ◯ 8 tens = 80

5. 
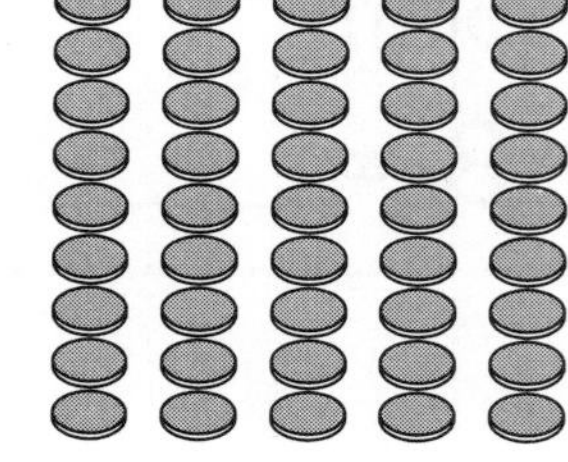

- ◯ 4 tens = 40
- ◯ 5 tens = 50
- ◯ 6 tens = 60
- ◯ 7 tens = 70

Name ______________________________

LESSON 13.2

# Tens and Ones to 20

Draw a picture.
Write the number.

1. Jack has 10 stickers. He finds 4 more. How many stickers does he have?

   14 stickers

2. Fran has 60 stickers. She puts 10 stickers on each page. How many pages does she fill?

   _____ pages

3. Tonya has 10 stickers. She finds 8 more. How many stickers does she have?

   _____ stickers

How many tens and ones?
Mark the correct answer.

4. 

- ◯ 0 tens 3 ones
- ◯ 1 ten 0 ones
- ◯ 1 ten 3 ones
- ◯ 0 tens 1 one

5. 

- ◯ 1 ten 7 ones
- ◯ 1 ten 6 ones
- ◯ 1 ten 8 ones
- ◯ 0 tens 7 ones

Name ______________________________



# Tens and Ones to 50

Draw a picture.
Solve.

| | |
|---|---|
| 1. Mrs. Hall has 3 boxes of 10 cookies. She buys 4 more cookies. How many cookies in all? <br> 34 cookies | |
| 2. Polly has 4 rolls of 10 mints. She buys 6 more mints. How many mints in all? <br> ______ mints | |
| 3. Suzy has 1 package of 10 crackers. She buys 7 more crackers. How many crackers in all? <br> ______ crackers | |

How many? Mark the correct answer.

4. 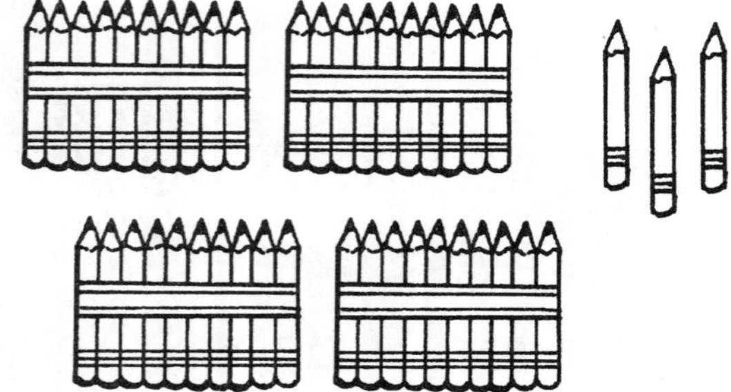

◯ 33 ◯ 34
◯ 43 ◯ 44

5. 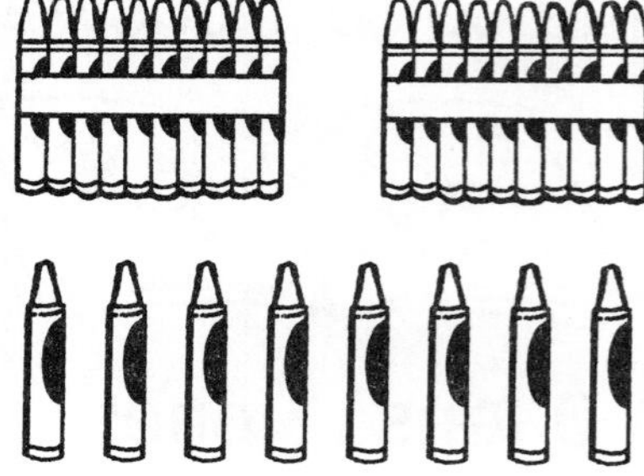

◯ 18 ◯ 23
◯ 25 ◯ 28

Name ______________________________



# Tens and Ones to 80

Draw a picture.
Write the number.

1. Bob spins 6 tens and 4 ones. What number does Bob spin?

   64

2. Marta spins 4 tens and 9 ones. What number does Marta spin?

   ______

3. Jimmy spins 7 tens and 6 ones. What number does Jimmy spin?

   ______

What is the number?
Mark the correct answer.

4. I have 6 tens.
   I have 8 ones.
   What number am I?

   ○ 61　○ 68
   ○ 81　○ 86

5. I have 7 tens.
   I have 2 ones.
   What number am I?

   ○ 27　○ 52
   ○ 70　○ 72

Name ______________________________



# Tens and Ones to 100

Draw a picture.
Write the number.

1. Bill packed 8 boxes of 10 books.
He found 3 more books.
How many books in all?

83 books

2. Molly packed 4 boxes of 10 cards.
She found 9 more cards.
How many cards in all?

_____ cards

Mark the correct answer.

3. What number does Chris show?

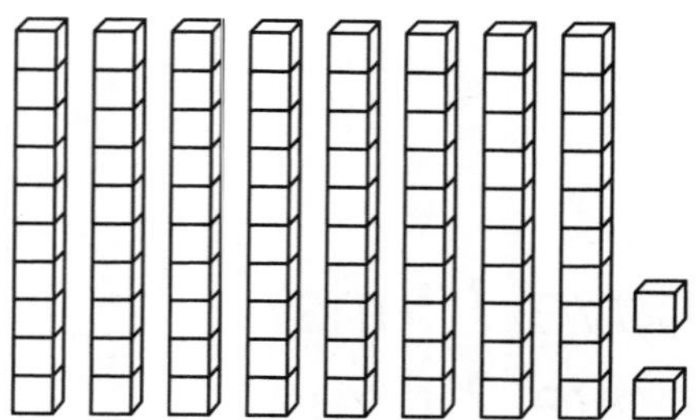

◯ 28 ◯ 72
◯ 82 ◯ 83

4. What number does Laura show?

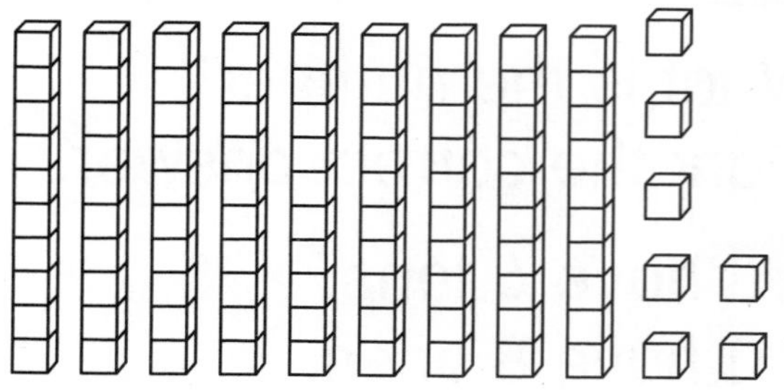

◯ 77 ◯ 79
◯ 87 ◯ 97

Name ______________________________

# Reading Strategy • Use Word Clues

Using word clues such as **more** and **fewer** can help you use pictures to estimate.

Look at the sheep.
Which is the better estimate?

more than 10 fewer than 10

---

1. Read the problem. Think about the meaning of **more** and **fewer**.

more than 10

10

fewer than 10

---

2. Estimate the number of sheep.

Think: 1 group of 10 sheep and 3 more sheep.
There are **more than 10** sheep.

---

Circle the better estimate.

3. 

more than 10

fewer than 10

4. 

more than 10

fewer than 10

Name ______________________________



# Ordinals

Use the picture to find the answer.

1. Lynn takes the seventh animal to school. What animal does she take?

2. Lynn counts all the animals that come after the third animal. How many are there?

______________________

3. Lynn adds a toy frog at the end of the line. In what position is the frog?

______________________

4. Lynn puts a toy cow between the duck and the hen. In what position is the hen now?

______________________

Mark the correct answer.

5. The winner in a race crosses the finish line _____.

   ◯ first ◯ second
   ◯ third ◯ fourth

6. There are nine seats left in a movie theater. You are the tenth in line. Will you get a seat?

   ◯ yes ◯ no

Name ________________________



# Greater Than

Draw a picture.
Write the correct answer.

1. Ann bakes 24 cookies.
   Leon bakes 36 cookies.
   Who bakes the greater number?

   Leon

2. Nick sells 12 cupcakes.
   Todd sells 21 cupcakes.
   Who sells the greater number?

   ________________

3. There are 3 people in line. Ted is behind Sally. Lou is behind Ted. Who is first in line?

   ________________

Mark the correct answer.

4. Which number is greater than 50?

   ◯ 5 ◯ 51
   ◯ 15 ◯ 50

5. Which number is greater than your age?

   ◯ 0 ◯ 4
   ◯ 2 ◯ 10

Name ______________________



# Less Than

Draw a picture.
Write the correct answer.

1. Jean has 32 toy cars. Luke has 23 cars. Which number is less?

   23

2. Paul uses 65 blocks. Renee uses 56. Who uses the greater number of blocks?

   ______________________

3. Marcy has 90 blocks. She makes 1 fence with 10 blocks. How many fences can she make?

   ______ fences

Mark the correct answer.

4. Which number is less than 46?
   - ◯ 45
   - ◯ 46
   - ◯ 48
   - ◯ 49

5. Which number is less than 11?
   - ◯ 9
   - ◯ 19
   - ◯ 29
   - ◯ 39

Name ____________________

LESSON 14.4

# Before, After, Between

Write the number.

1. Kay chooses a number between 75 and 77. What number does she choose?

   76

2. Which number is greater than 35?

   31 16 45 27

   ______

3. Kerry finished the race before Tom. Sally finished the race after Tom. Who finished the race first?

   ______________________

Mark the correct answer.

4. Which number is just after 54?

   ◯ 55 ◯ 52
   ◯ 53 ◯ 51

5. Which number is just before 40?

   ◯ 29 ◯ 39
   ◯ 35 ◯ 41

Name ______________________



# Order to 100

Look at the picture.
Write the numbers from least to greatest.

1. Mary wants to put these hats in order from least to greatest.

12 22 62 82

2. Sam wants to put these balls in order from least to greatest.

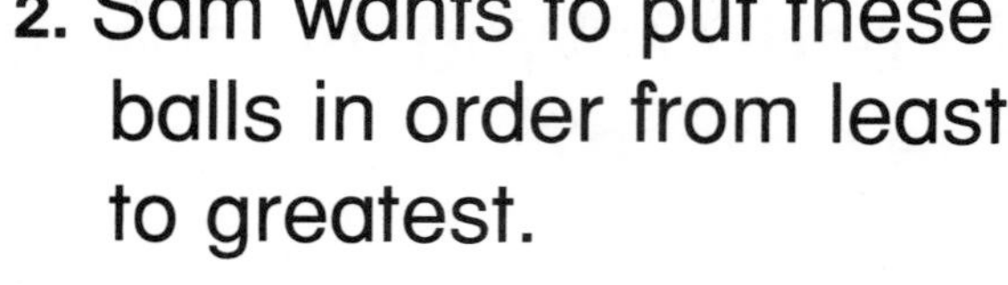

____ ____ ____ ____

Write the correct answer.

3. Chet picks three number cards. The numbers are between 40 and 44. What numbers does he pick?

____ ____ ____

4. Nan picks three number cards. The numbers are after 34 but before 38. What numbers does she pick?

____ ____ ____

Mark the correct answer.

5. Which numbers are in order from least to greatest?

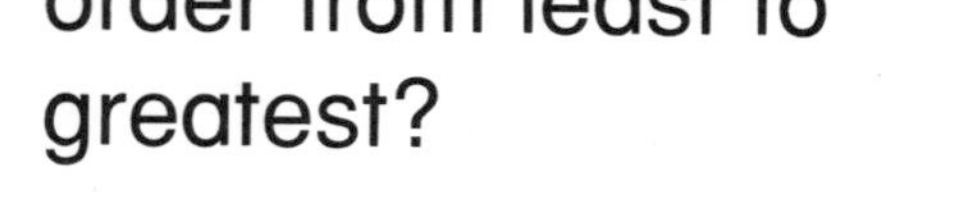

- ○ 12, 37, 39, 42
- ○ 12, 39, 37, 42
- ○ 42, 39, 37, 12

6. Which set of cards is in order from least to greatest?

- ○ 29 | 20 | 23
- ○ 23 | 20 | 29
- ○ 20 | 23 | 29

Name ____________________



# Counting by Tens

Draw a picture.
Count by tens.

1. There are 4 children in a family. Each child gets 10 dollars for a present. How much money do they get in all?

 40 dollars

2. Carlos has 7 packs of baseball cards. Each pack has 10 cards. How many cards does he have in all?

 ______ cards

Mark the correct answer.

3. What three numbers come next in this pattern?

 20, 30, 40, ___, ___, ___

 ◯ 41, 42, 43
 ◯ 45, 50, 55
 ◯ 60, 70, 80
 ◯ 50, 60, 70

4. How many in all?

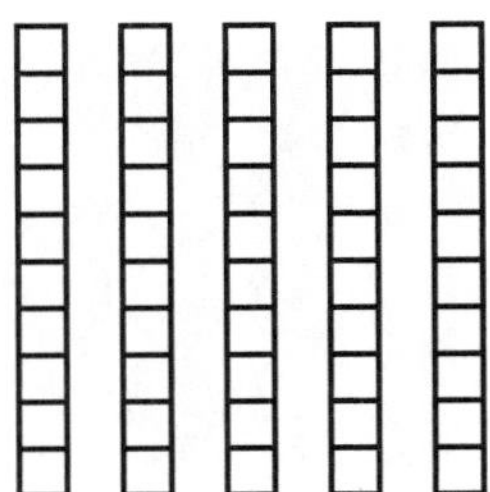

 ◯ 5
 ◯ 40
 ◯ 50
 ◯ 60

Name ______________________________



# Counting by Fives

Draw a picture.
Skip-count to solve.

1. Hannah is 6 years old today. Her grandmother gives her 5 dollars for each year. How much money does Hannah get?

   30 dollars

2. Tory builds 8 towers. He uses 10 blocks in each tower. How many blocks does Tory use in all?

   ______ blocks

Mark the correct answer.

3. How many in all?

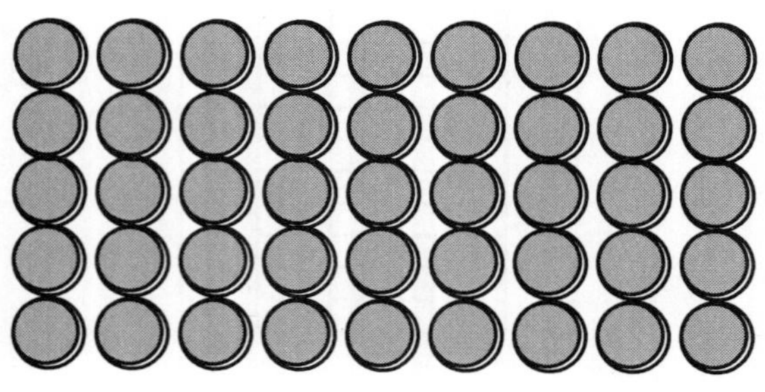

- ◯ 9
- ◯ 40
- ◯ 45
- ◯ 90

4. What three numbers come next in this pattern?

   55, 60, 65, ___, ___, ___

- ◯ 80, 85, 90
- ◯ 75, 80, 85
- ◯ 70, 80, 90
- ◯ 70, 75, 80

Name ______________________________



# Counting by Twos

Draw a picture.
Skip-count to solve.

1. Doug thinks of a number.
   It is between 35 and 40.
   It is 2 more than 36.
   What is Doug's number?

   38

2. Sal thinks of a number.
   It is between 70 and 80.
   It is 5 more than 70.
   What is Sal's number?

   ______

Mark the correct answer.

3. When you say every second number, you are counting by ______.

   - ◯ twos
   - ◯ fives
   - ◯ tens

4. What three numbers come next in this pattern?

   52, 54, 56, ___, ___, ___

   - ◯ 57, 59, 61
   - ◯ 58, 60, 62
   - ◯ 60, 65, 70

Name ________________________



# Even and Odd Numbers

Draw a picture to solve.
Then circle **odd** or **even.**

1. Marissa plants 5 flowers. She plants 3 more. How many flowers does she plant?

   8 flowers odd (even)

2. Bill mows 3 lawns on Monday. He mows double that number on Tuesday. How many lawns does he mow on both days?

   ______ lawns odd even

3. 6 children each plant 2 bulbs. How many bulbs do they plant in all?

   ______ bulbs odd even

Mark the correct answer.

4. The sum of an even number and an odd number is always ______.

   ○ even ○ odd

5. The sum of two odd numbers is always ______.

   ○ even ○ odd

Name ______________________



# Pennies and Nickels

Draw a picture. Count.
Write the amount.

1. Lisa has 2 pennies.
   She finds 3 more pennies in a jar.
   How much money does Lisa have in all?

   5 ¢

2. Bob has 2 nickels.
   His mom gives him 1 more nickel.
   How much money does he have in all?

   _____ ¢

Mark the correct answer.

3. Which group of coins is worth more?

   ◯ 6 pennies

   ◯ 2 nickels

   ◯ 11 pennies

4. Hanna wants to count her coins. What should she say?

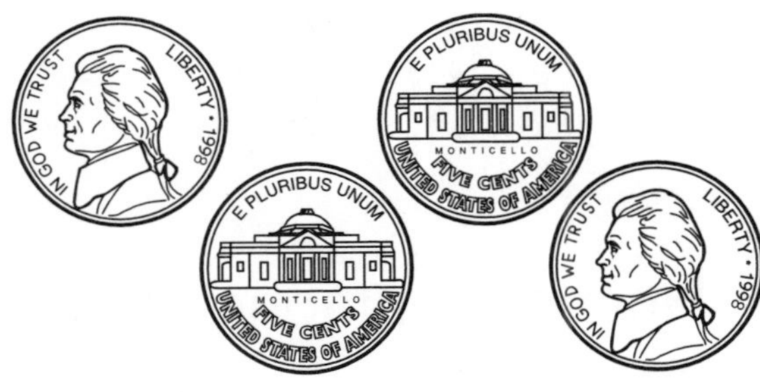


   ◯ 1¢, 2¢, 3¢, 4¢

   ◯ 5¢, 10¢, 15¢

   ◯ 5¢, 10¢, 15¢, 20¢

Name ______________________________



# Pennies and Dimes

Draw a picture. Count.
Write the amount.

1. Ned has 4 dimes.
He earns 2 more dimes.
How much money does Ned have in all?

¢

2. Patty has 2 nickels.
She earns 3 more nickels.
How much money does she have in all?

______¢

Mark the correct answer.

3. Mary has these coins.

How much money does she have?

- ◯ 2¢
- ◯ 10¢
- ◯ 15¢
- ◯ 20¢

4. Ben wants to count his coins. What should he say?

- ◯ 1¢, 2¢, 3¢
- ◯ 5¢, 10¢, 15¢
- ◯ 10¢, 20¢, 30¢
- ◯ not here

Name ______________________



# Counting Collections of Nickels and Pennies

Draw a picture. Count.
Write the amount.

1. Dan has 3 nickels in his bank.
He puts in 4 pennies.
How much money does Dan have in all?

19 ¢

2. Jessica has 2 dimes.
Her aunt gives her 3 more dimes.
How much money does Jessica have in all?

_____ ¢

Mark the correct answer.

3. Which group of coins is worth the most?

- ○ 3 nickels and 3 pennies
- ○ 2 nickels and 9 pennies
- ○ 4 nickels and 1 penny
- ○ 3 nickels and 7 pennies

4. Which amount do these coins add up to?

- ○ 10¢
- ○ 12¢
- ○ 22¢
- ○ not here

Name ______________________________



# Counting Collections of Dimes and Pennies

Draw a picture. Count.
Write the amount.

1. Katie has 3 dimes. Her mom puts 2 more dimes in her lunch box. How much money does Katie have in all?

   50 ¢

2. John has 4 nickels in his bank. He puts in 4 pennies. How much money does he have in all?

   ______¢

Mark the correct answer.

3. Which group of coins is worth the least?

   ◯ 12 pennies
   ◯ 1 dime 1 penny
   ◯ 1 dime 4 pennies
   ◯ 2 dimes

4. What amount do these coins add up to?

   ◯ 5¢ ◯ 13¢
   ◯ 23¢ ◯ 50¢

Name ____________________



# Reading Strategy • Use Pictures

Using pictures can help you solve problems.

A toy truck costs 21¢. Which coins could Thomas use to buy the truck?

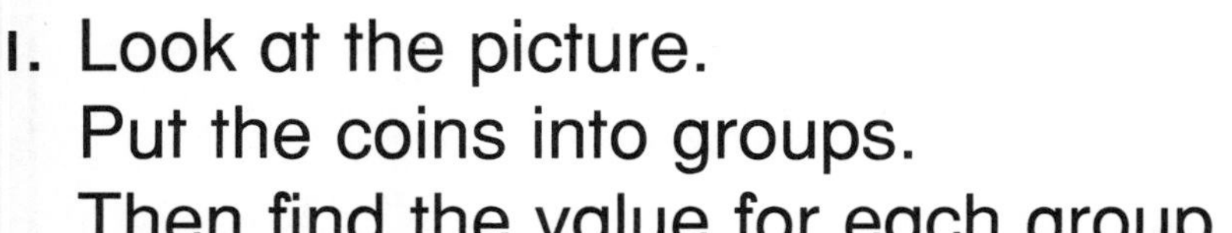

1. Look at the picture. Put the coins into groups. Then find the value for each group.

| dimes | nickels | pennies |
|---|---|---|
| 20 ¢ | 10 ¢ | 2 ¢ |

2. Write the number of coins from the groups that add up to the price of the toy truck.

1 dime 2 nickels 1 penny = 21 ¢

Solve.

3.    

A toy bus costs 12¢. Which coins could you use to buy it?

_____ dime

_____ nickels

_____ pennies

Name ______________________________



# Trading Pennies, Nickels, and Dimes

Use the fewest coins.
Draw the coins.
Solve.

1. Mrs. Polt needs dimes for parking. She has 20 pennies and 2 nickels. How many dimes can she trade for?

   __3__ dimes

2. Mr. Miller uses dimes and nickels for tolls. He has 35 pennies. How many dimes and nickels can he trade for?

   _____ dimes _____ nickel

Mark the correct answer.

3. What are the fewest coins you can use to show 25¢?

   ◯ 2 coins
   ◯ 3 coins
   ◯ 5 coins
   ◯ 25 coins

4. Tina has 4 coins. José has 8 coins. Who has more money?

   ◯ Tina
   ◯ José
   ◯ You cannot tell.

Name ______________________________



# Equal Amounts

Draw a picture.
Write the amount.

1. Jill buys jacks that cost 30¢. Show two ways she could pay.

   __ dimes __ nickels __ pennies

   __ dimes __ nickels __ pennies

2. Alex buys a ball that costs 45¢. Show two ways he could pay.

   __ dimes __ nickels __ pennies

   __ dimes __ nickels __ pennies

Mark the correct answer.

3. Betty and Frank have the same amount of money. Betty has only dimes. Frank has only nickels. Who has fewer coins?

   ◯ Betty

   ◯ Frank

   ◯ You cannot tell.

4. Joe and Carmen have the same number of coins. Do they have the same amount of money?

   ◯ yes

   ◯ no

   ◯ You cannot tell.

Name ____________________



# How Much Is Needed?

Draw a picture.
Solve.

1. Nicky has 22¢ in her purse. She has 4 coins. What are they?

2 dimes 0 nickels 2 pennies

2. Don has 1 dime and 7 nickels. Lisa has the same amount but fewer coins. What coins does she have?

__ dimes __ nickel

Mark the correct answer.

3. Ted uses fewer coins than Janna to show the same amount. This means that some of Ted's coins are worth ______.

- ◯ more
- ◯ less
- ◯ the same

4. A cookie costs 15¢. Joe uses the fewest coins to buy it. What coins does he use?

- ◯ 15 pennies
- ◯ 2 nickels and 5 pennies
- ◯ 3 nickels
- ◯ 1 dime and 1 nickel

Name ____________________



# Quarter

Draw a picture. Count.
Write the amount.

1. Fran has 1 quarter.
   She earns 1 dime and 1 nickel.
   How much money does Fran have in all?

   40 ¢

2. Pete has 2 dimes.
   He finds 1 more dime and 2 nickels in his bag. How much money does Pete have in all?

   ____ ¢

Mark the correct answer.

3. Which group of coins is worth the most?

   ◯ 1 quarter and 2 dimes

   ◯ 1 quarter and 3 nickels

   ◯ 1 quarter and 5 nickels

   ◯ 1 quarter and 20 pennies

4. What amount do these coins add up to?

   ◯ 36¢ ◯ 39¢

   ◯ 41¢ ◯ 46¢

Name ___________________________



# Reading Strategy • Make Predictions

Making predictions can help you solve problems.

A toy plane costs 37¢. Charlie has 1 quarter, 1 dime, 1 nickel, and 1 penny. Does Charlie have enough to buy the plane?

1. Use coins to show the amount Charlie has. Count two coins.

25 ¢, 35 ¢

2. Make a prediction. Do you think Charlie has enough to buy the plane? yes

3. Continue counting Charlie's coins to find the value.

_____ ¢, _____ ¢, _____ ¢, _____ ¢

Make a prediction. Then solve. Use the fewest coins.

4. A toy bear costs 37¢. Jill has 2 dimes, 5 nickels, and 3 pennies. Can Jill buy the plane? If so, what coins should she use?

_____ dimes

_____ nickels

_____ pennies

Name ______________________________

LESSON 18.1

# Ordering Months and Days

**January**

| S | M | T | W | T | F | S |
|---|---|---|---|---|---|---|
| | | | | 1 | 2 | 3 |
| 4 | 5 | 6 | 7 | 8 | 9 | 10 |
| 11 | 12 | 13 | 14 | 15 | 16 | 17 |
| 18 | 19 | 20 | 21 | 22 | 23 | 24 |
| 25 | 26 | 27 | 28 | 29 | 30 | 31 |

**February**

| S | M | T | W | T | F | S |
|---|---|---|---|---|---|---|
| 1 | 2 | 3 | 4 | 5 | 6 | 7 |
| 8 | 9 | 10 | 11 | 12 | 13 | 14 |
| 15 | 16 | 17 | 18 | 19 | 20 | 21 |
| 22 | 23 | 24 | 25 | 26 | 27 | 28 |

**March**

| S | M | T | W | T | F | S |
|---|---|---|---|---|---|---|
| 1 | 2 | 3 | 4 | 5 | 6 | 7 |
| 8 | 9 | 10 | 11 | 12 | 13 | 14 |
| 15 | 16 | 17 | 18 | 19 | 20 | 21 |
| 22 | 23 | 24 | 25 | 26 | 27 | 28 |
| 29 | 30 | 31 | | | | |

**April**

| S | M | T | W | T | F | S |
|---|---|---|---|---|---|---|
| | | | 1 | 2 | 3 | 4 |
| 5 | 6 | 7 | 8 | 9 | 10 | 11 |
| 12 | 13 | 14 | 15 | 16 | 17 | 18 |
| 19 | 20 | 21 | 22 | 23 | 24 | 25 |
| 26 | 27 | 28 | 29 | 30 | | |

**May**

| S | M | T | W | T | F | S |
|---|---|---|---|---|---|---|
| | | | | | 1 | 2 |
| 3 | 4 | 5 | 6 | 7 | 8 | 9 |
| 10 | 11 | 12 | 13 | 14 | 15 | 16 |
| 17 | 18 | 19 | 20 | 21 | 22 | 23 |
| 24/31 | 25 | 26 | 27 | 28 | 29 | 30 |

**June**

| S | M | T | W | T | F | S |
|---|---|---|---|---|---|---|
| | 1 | 2 | 3 | 4 | 5 | 6 |
| 7 | 8 | 9 | 10 | 11 | 12 | 13 |
| 14 | 15 | 16 | 17 | 18 | 19 | 20 |
| 21 | 22 | 23 | 24 | 25 | 26 | 27 |
| 28 | 29 | 30 | | | | |

**July**

| S | M | T | W | T | F | S |
|---|---|---|---|---|---|---|
| | | | 1 | 2 | 3 | 4 |
| 5 | 6 | 7 | 8 | 9 | 10 | 11 |
| 12 | 13 | 14 | 15 | 16 | 17 | 18 |
| 19 | 20 | 21 | 22 | 23 | 24 | 25 |
| 26 | 27 | 28 | 29 | 30 | 31 | |

**August**

| S | M | T | W | T | F | S |
|---|---|---|---|---|---|---|
| | | | | | | 1 |
| 2 | 3 | 4 | 5 | 6 | 7 | 8 |
| 9 | 10 | 11 | 12 | 13 | 14 | 15 |
| 16 | 17 | 18 | 19 | 20 | 21 | 22 |
| 23/30 | 24/31 | 25 | 26 | 27 | 28 | 29 |

**September**

| S | M | T | W | T | F | S |
|---|---|---|---|---|---|---|
| | | 1 | 2 | 3 | 4 | 5 |
| 6 | 7 | 8 | 9 | 10 | 11 | 12 |
| 13 | 14 | 15 | 16 | 17 | 18 | 19 |
| 20 | 21 | 22 | 23 | 24 | 25 | 26 |
| 27 | 28 | 29 | 30 | | | |

**October**

| S | M | T | W | T | F | S |
|---|---|---|---|---|---|---|
| | | | | 1 | 2 | 3 |
| 4 | 5 | 6 | 7 | 8 | 9 | 10 |
| 11 | 12 | 13 | 14 | 15 | 16 | 17 |
| 18 | 19 | 20 | 21 | 22 | 23 | 24 |
| 25 | 26 | 27 | 28 | 29 | 30 | 31 |

**November**

| S | M | T | W | T | F | S |
|---|---|---|---|---|---|---|
| 1 | 2 | 3 | 4 | 5 | 6 | 7 |
| 8 | 9 | 10 | 11 | 12 | 13 | 14 |
| 15 | 16 | 17 | 18 | 19 | 20 | 21 |
| 22 | 23 | 24 | 25 | 26 | 27 | 28 |
| 29 | 30 | | | | | |

**December**

| S | M | T | W | T | F | S |
|---|---|---|---|---|---|---|
| | | 1 | 2 | 3 | 4 | 5 |
| 6 | 7 | 8 | 9 | 10 | 11 | 12 |
| 13 | 14 | 15 | 16 | 17 | 18 | 19 |
| 20 | 21 | 22 | 23 | 24 | 25 | 26 |
| 27 | 28 | 29 | 30 | 31 | | |

Use the calendar to answer each question.

1. Ann's birthday is in the third month of the year. In what month is her birthday?

   March

2. Tom's birthday comes in the month after June. In what month is Tom's birthday?

   ______________________

3. What is the month before December?

   ______________________

4. What is the ninth month of the year?

   ______________________

Mark the correct answer.

5. How many months are there in one year?
   - ◯ 10 months
   - ◯ 11 months
   - ◯ 12 months
   - ◯ not here

6. What month comes between May and July?
   - ◯ April
   - ◯ June
   - ◯ August
   - ◯ not here

Name ______________________________



# Reading Strategy • Matching Text

Looking for matching words can help you solve a problem.

Jon has a game on the second Monday of November. On what date is the game?

| November | | | | | | |
|---|---|---|---|---|---|---|
| SUN. | MON. | TUES. | WED. | THURS. | FRI. | SAT |
| | 1 | 2 | 3 | 4 | 5 | 6 |
| 7 | 8 | 9 | 10 | 11 | 12 | 13 |
| 14 | 15 | 16 | 17 | 18 | 19 | 20 |
| 21 | 22 | 23 | 24 | 25 | 26 | 27 |
| 28 | 29 | 30 | | | | |

1. Read the problem. What date do you need to find?

2. Match words from the problem with words on the calendar. Find **Monday** in the list of days at the top of the calendar.

3. Find the second Monday on the calendar. What is the date?

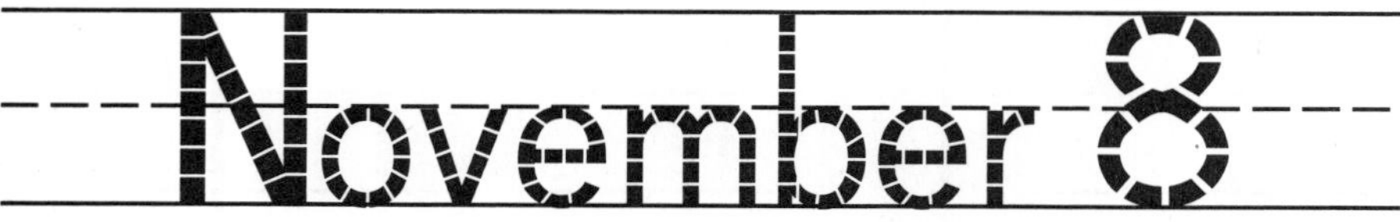


Use the calendar to answer the questions.

4. Linda's party is the third Tuesday of November. On what date is the party?

______________________

5. Thanksgiving is the fourth Thursday of November. On what date is Thanksgiving?

______________________

Name ____________________

LESSON 18.3

# Ordering Events

Read each story.
Write **morning, afternoon,** or **evening** to tell the time.

1. Luis is hungry after school. He eats an apple for a snack. Then he goes outside to play.

   afternoon

2. Sally takes too much time getting dressed. After breakfast, she must run to catch the school bus.

   ____________________

3. Marta takes the bus to her music teacher's house. She gets home before it is dark.

   ____________________

4. Tammy puts on her pajamas. Then she reads a story before going to sleep.

   ____________________

Mark the correct answer.

5. Which do most people do in the evening?

   ◯ eat breakfast
   ◯ eat lunch
   ◯ eat dinner

6. When does this happen?

   ◯ in the morning
   ◯ in the afternoon
   ◯ in the evening

Name ___________________________________

LESSON 18.4

# Reading Strategy • Use Prior Knowledge

How much time do these things take to do?
Number them from the shortest time to the longest time.

Leslie makes her bed.

2

Leslie hangs up her coat.

1

Leslie eats dinner.

3

---

1. Read each sentence.
   About how long does it take you to do each thing?

   It takes a very short time to hang up a coat.
   It takes a longer time to make a bed.
   It takes the longest time to eat dinner.

---

Number these things from the shortest time to the longest time. Use 1, 2, 3.

2. Mark gets ready for bed.
   He takes a bath.
   He brushes his hair.
   He brushes his teeth.

_____ He takes a bath.

_____ He brushes his hair.

_____ He brushes his teeth.

Name ___________________________________



# Reading the Clock

Use the clock.
Write the time two ways.

1. Alice catches the school bus at

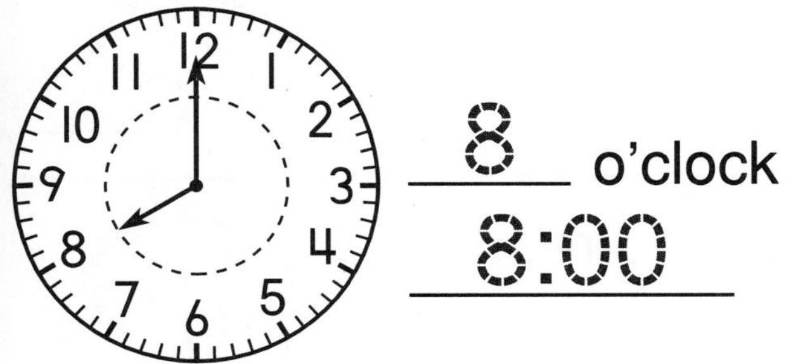

8 o'clock
8:00

2. John has math at

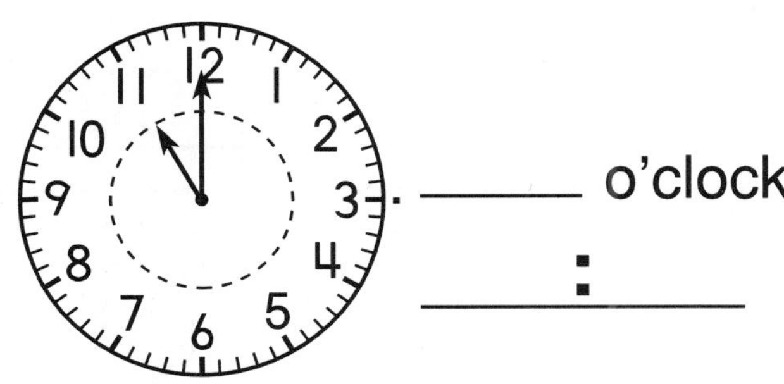

_____ o'clock
_____ : _____

3. Sam has gym at

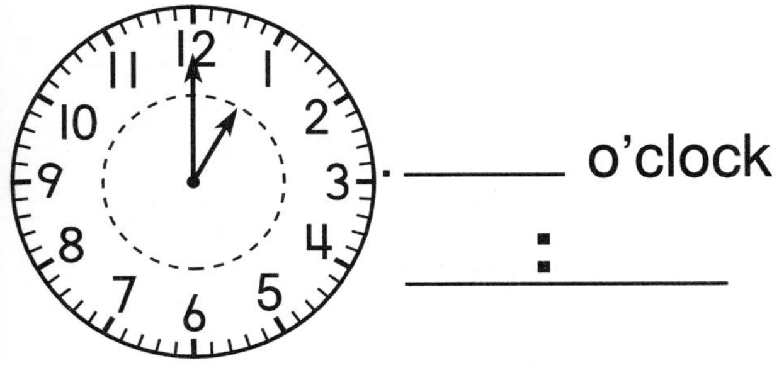

_____ o'clock
_____ : _____

4. Polly eats dinner at

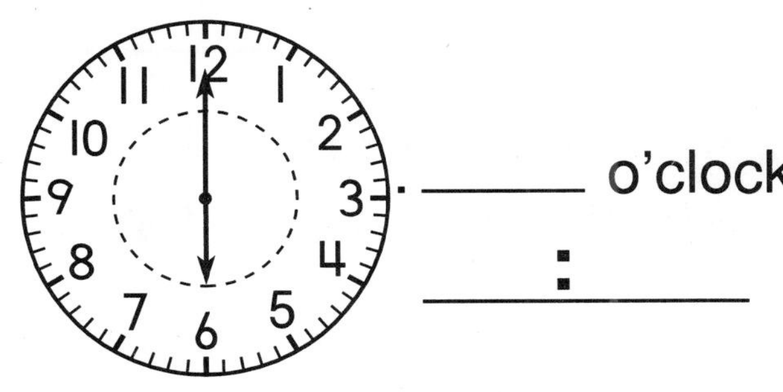

_____ o'clock
_____ : _____

Mark the correct answer.

5. What time is it?

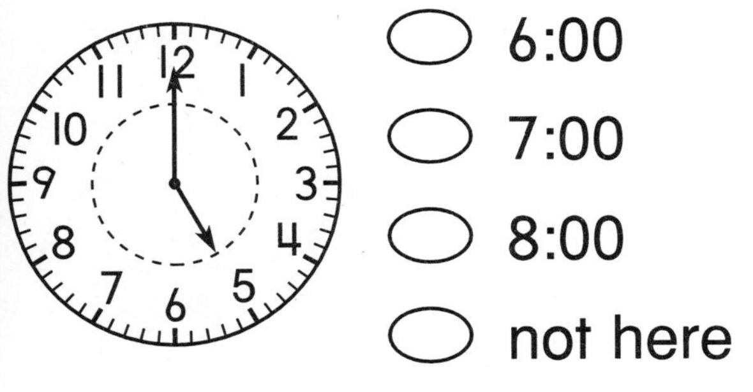

- ◯ 6:00
- ◯ 7:00
- ◯ 8:00
- ◯ not here

6. What time will it be in **two hours**?

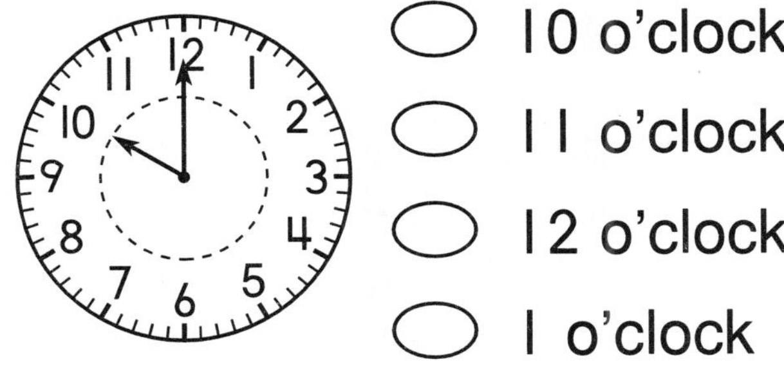

- ◯ 10 o'clock
- ◯ 11 o'clock
- ◯ 12 o'clock
- ◯ 1 o'clock

Name ___________________________________



# Hour

Write the time.

1. Mrs. Lee will see the dentist at

2:00.

2. The station clock says

___:___.

3. Nora rode her bike at

___:___.

4. Ted read a book at

___:___.

Mark the correct answer.

5. Which clock shows the same time?

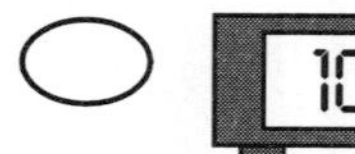

6. Which clock shows the same time?

Name ______________________________

LESSON 19.3

# Time to the Hour

Show the time.
Draw the hour hand and the minute hand.

1. Steve will go to the party at 2:00.

2. Mary will get home at 5:00.

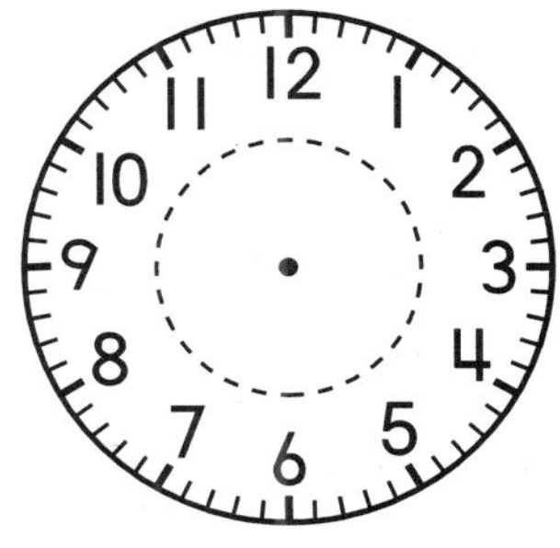

3. Mrs. Hill will go shopping at 4:00.

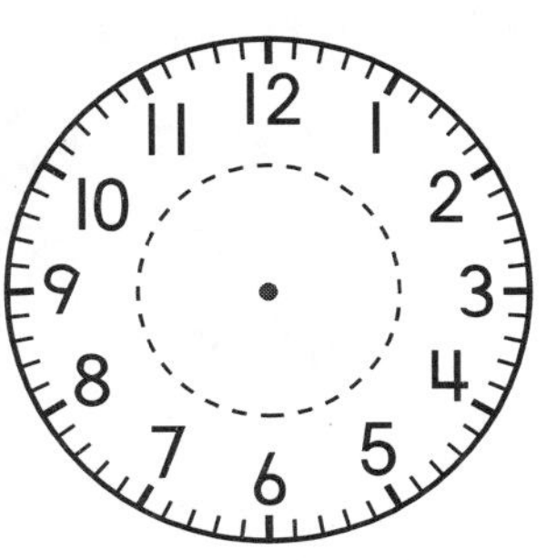

4. Dave goes to bed at 9:00.

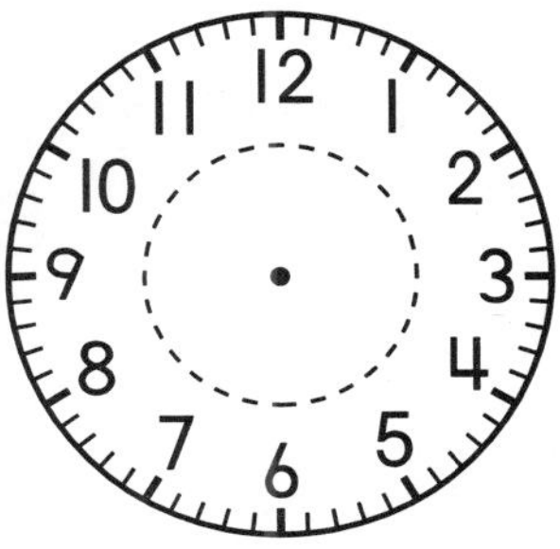

Mark the correct answer.

5. Read the clock. What time is it?

- ◯ 9 o'clock
- ◯ 10 o'clock
- ◯ 11 o'clock
- ◯ 12 o'clock

6. Which hand on a clock tells the hour?

- ◯ the short hand
- ◯ the long hand

Name ___________________________________________



# Half-Hour

Use a clock. Write the time.

1. Mel's favorite TV show starts at 7:30. It lasts half an hour. What time does it end?

   8:00

2. Sunny's dance class starts at 4:30. It lasts one hour. What time does it end?

   ____________

Draw the hour and the minute hands.

3. Cathy's music lesson begins at 3:00. It lasts one hour. Show the time it ends.

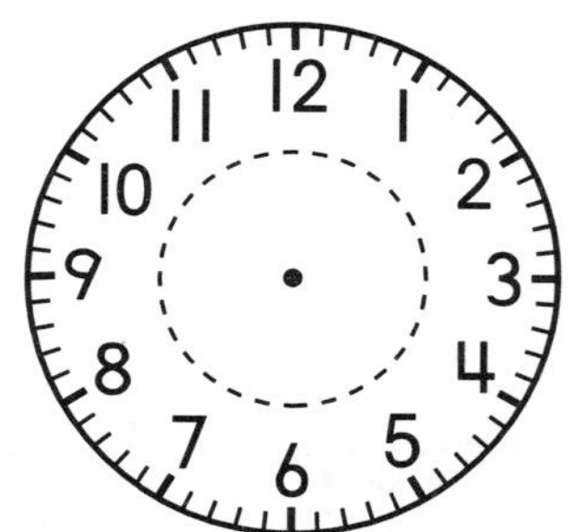

4. Barb starts to play a game at 10:00. It lasts 30 minutes. Show the time it ends.

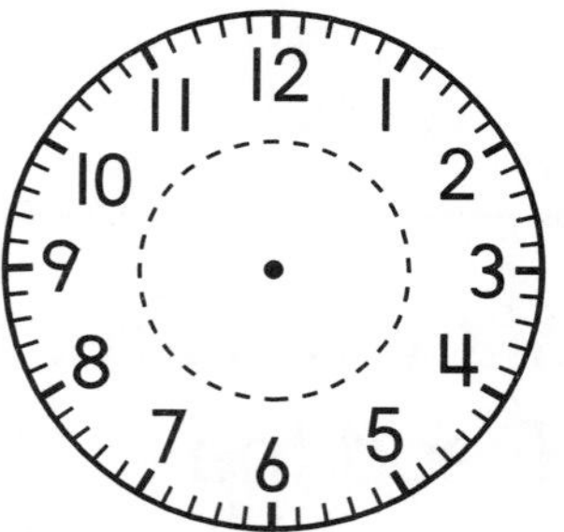

Mark the correct answer.

5. What time is it?

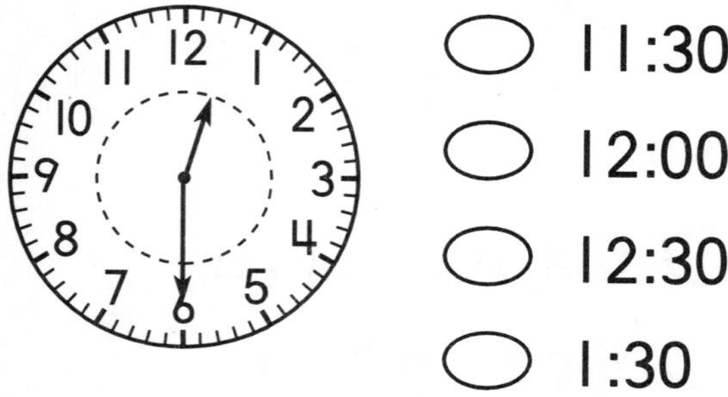

◯ 11:30
◯ 12:00
◯ 12:30
◯ 1:30

6. What time will it be in half an hour?

◯ 2:00
◯ 2:30
◯ 3:00
◯ not here

Name ______________________

LESSON 19.5

# Reading Strategy • Use Word Clues

Tina paints a big picture for her dad's birthday. About how long will it take to paint the picture?

more than 1 minute

less than 1 minute

1. Read the problem. Draw a line under what you want to find out.

---

2. Circle the word that tells about the picture.

---

3. Estimate how long it will take. Circle your estimate. Act out the problem to check if needed.

---

Read the problem. Look for clues to help you estimate. Circle your estimate. Then act it out if needed.

4. Tina signs a birthday card with her first name. About how long will it take?

   less than a minute

   more than a minute

5. Jim writes a long story about his party. About how long will it take?

   less than a minute

   more than a minute

Name ______________________



# Using Nonstandard Units

Draw a picture.
Write how many paper clips long.

1. Mark uses paper clips to measure his pencil. About how many paper clips long are 2 pencils?

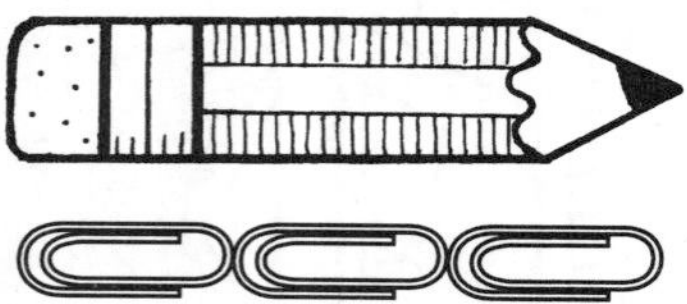

about 6 paper clips

2. Jan uses paper clips to measure a pin. About how many paper clips long are 3 pins?

about ______ paper clips

Mark the correct answer.

3. Dan's desk measures 29 paper clips long. Bill's desk measures 36 paper clips long. Who has the longer desk?

- ◯ Dan
- ◯ Bill

4. The length of Pam's shoe is 2 paper clips longer than Kim's shoe. Who has the longer shoe?

- ◯ Pam
- ◯ Kim

Name ______________________________



# Measuring in Inch Units

Color the inch units.
Write the number of inches.

1. Diane's ribbon is 6 inches long.
Kara's ribbon is 4 inches shorter.
How long is Kara's ribbon?

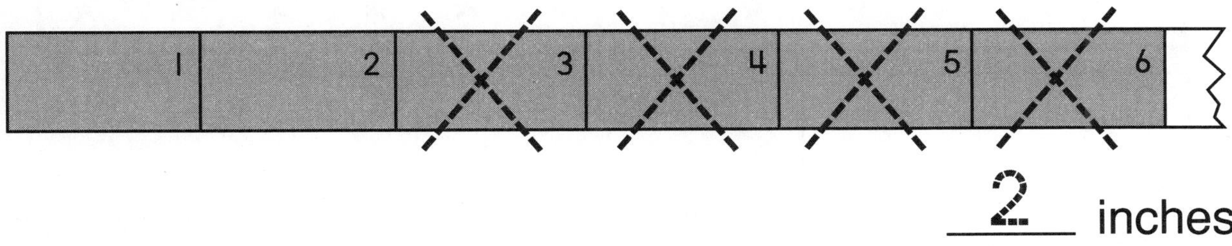


__2__ inches

---

2. Adam's string is 3 inches long.
Pat's string is 2 inches longer.
How long is Pat's string?

| 1 | 2 | 3 | 4 | 5 | 6 |
|---|---|---|---|---|---|

______ inches

---

Mark the correct answer.

3. Each link of a chain is 1 inch. The chain has 7 links. How long is the chain?

- ◯ 5 inches
- ◯ 6 inches
- ◯ 7 inches
- ◯ 8 inches

4. A toy robot takes 10 equal steps to walk a 10-inch line. How long is the robot's foot?

- ◯ 1 inch
- ◯ 2 inches
- ◯ 4 inches
- ◯ 5 inches

Name ______________________________

LESSON 20.3

# Using an Inch Ruler

Draw a line to show where to cut.

1. Sarah needs a ribbon 5 inches long. Draw a line to show where you would cut the ribbon.

| inches 1 | 2 | 3 | 4 | 5 | 6 |
|---|---|---|---|---|---|

2. Diane needs a piece of yarn 3 inches long. Draw a line to show where you would cut the yarn.

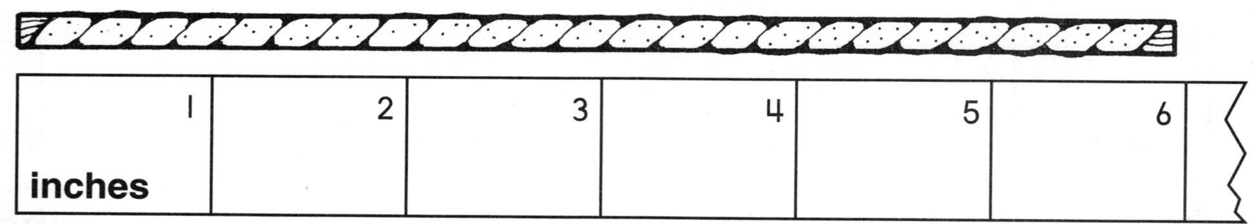


Mark the correct answer.

3. How long is it?

| inches 1 | 2 | 3 |
|---|---|---|

- ◯ 2 inches
- ◯ 1 inch
- ◯ 3 inches

4. How long is it?

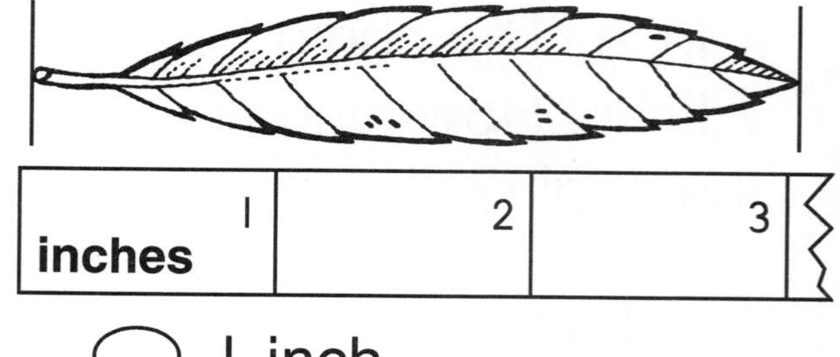


- ◯ 1 inch
- ◯ 2 inches
- ◯ 3 inches

Name ______________________________

LESSON 20.4

# Measuring in Centimeter Units

Color the centimeter units.
Write how many.

1. A crayon is 6 centimeters long.
   A rubber band is 2 centimeters shorter.
   How long is the rubber band?

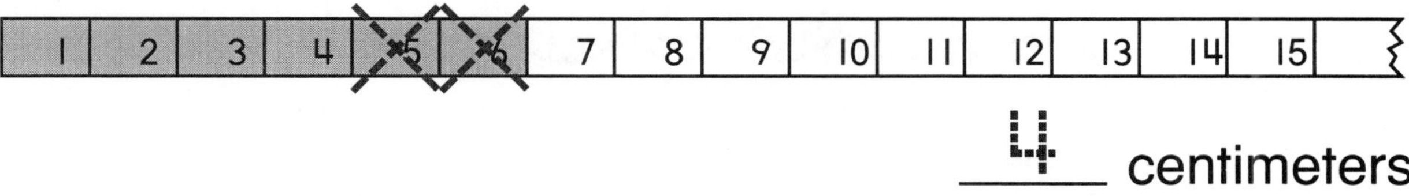


4 centimeters

---

2. A pen is 10 centimeters long.
   A marker is 2 centimeters longer.
   How long is the marker?

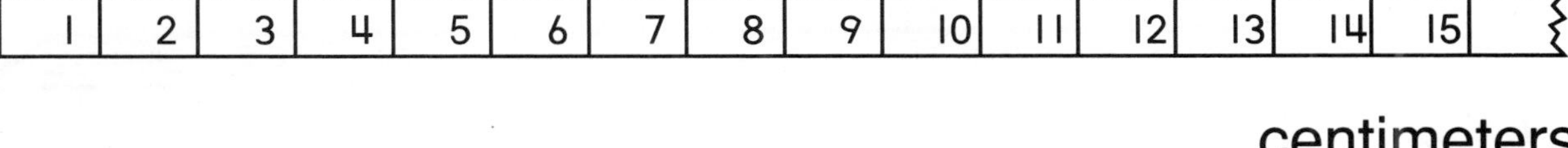


______ centimeters

---

Mark the correct answer.

3. How many inches long?

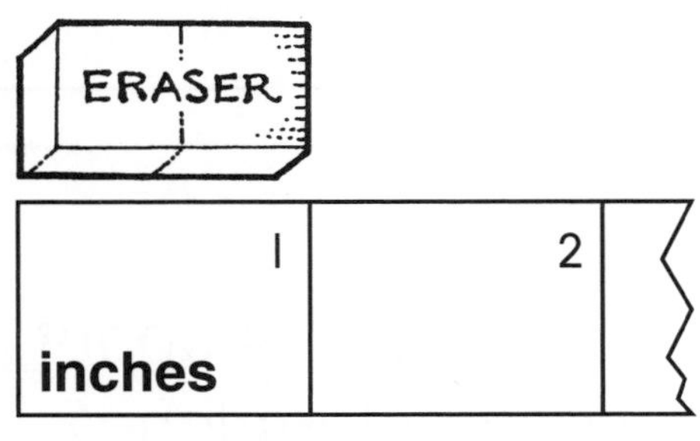


- ◯ 1 inch
- ◯ 2 inches
- ◯ 3 inches
- ◯ 4 inches

4. How many centimeters long?

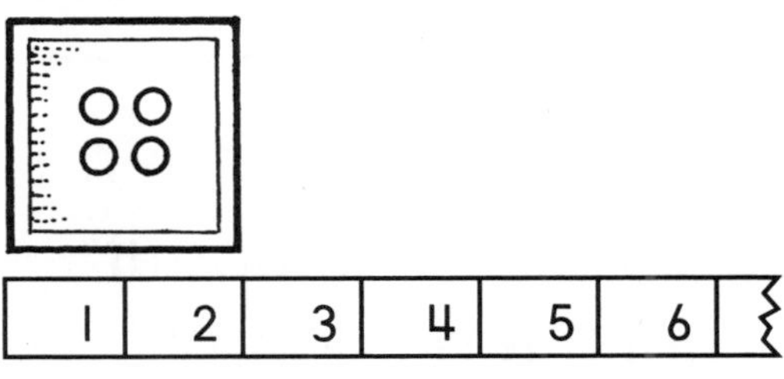


- ◯ 2 centimeters
- ◯ 3 centimeters
- ◯ 4 centimeters
- ◯ 5 centimeters

Name ____________________

LESSON 20.5

# Using a Centimeter Ruler

Draw a line to show the centimeters.

1. Mrs. Miller wants to cut 8 centimeters of lace.

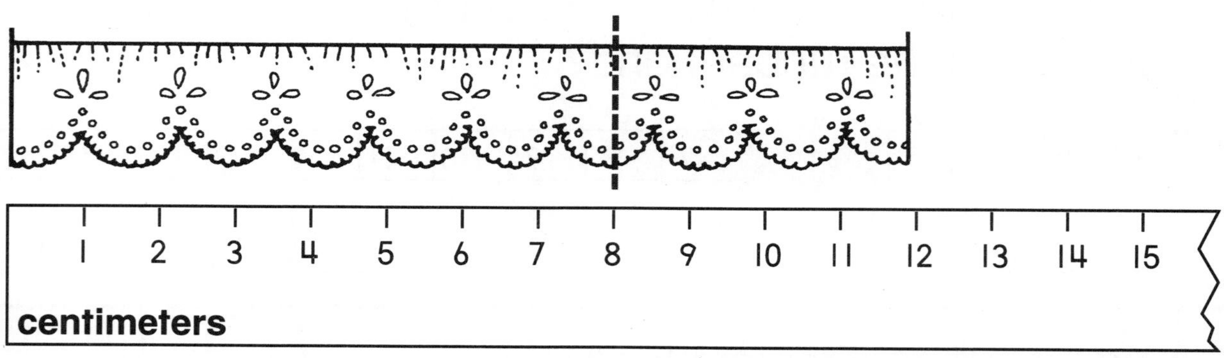


2. Mr. Polt wants to cut 12 centimeters of wood.

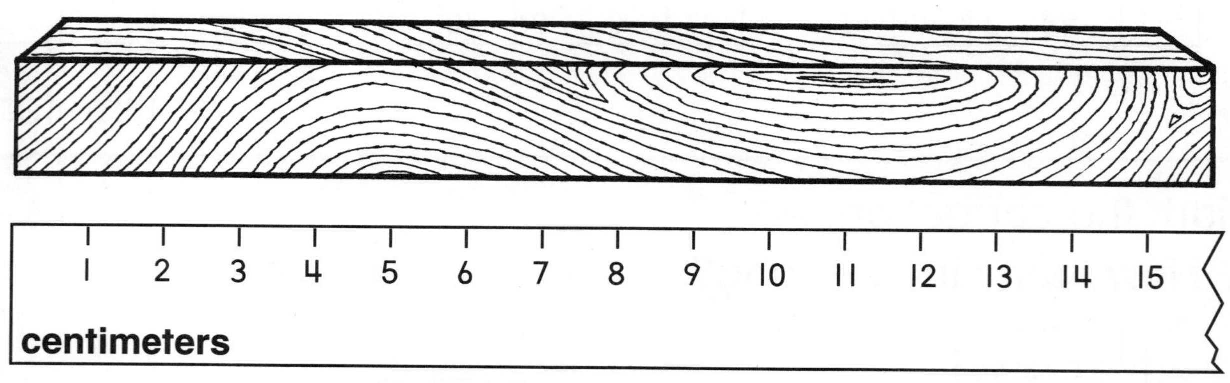


Mark the correct answer.

3. Which object is about 8 centimeters long?

   - ◯ your math book
   - ◯ a crayon
   - ◯ a paper clip

4. Which object is about 15 centimeters long?

   - ◯ a paintbrush
   - ◯ a key
   - ◯ a safety pin

Name ______________________________

LESSON 21.1

# Using a Balance

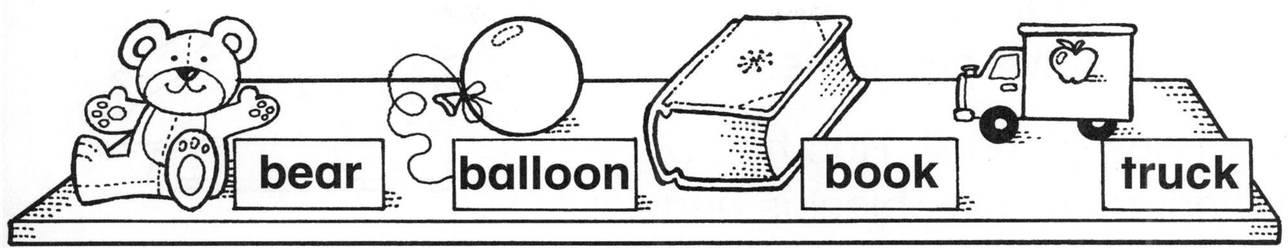


Use the picture. Write the answer.

1. Leslie takes something to share for show-and-tell. She chooses the heaviest object on the shelf.

   What does she choose?

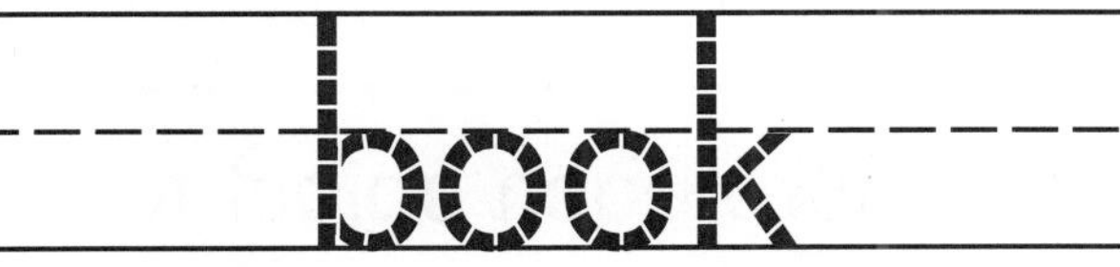


2. Rob takes something to share for show-and-tell. He chooses the lightest object on the shelf.

   What does he choose? ______________________

Mark the correct answer.

3. A paper clip is heavier than a pin. A penny is heavier than a paper clip. Which object is heaviest?

   ◯ paper clip

   ◯ pin

   ◯ penny

4. A shoe is lighter than a book. A tube of paint is lighter than a shoe. Which object is lightest?

   ◯ shoe

   ◯ book

   ◯ tube of paint

Name ______________________________



# Reading Strategy • Make a Prediction

Making predictions can help you solve problems.

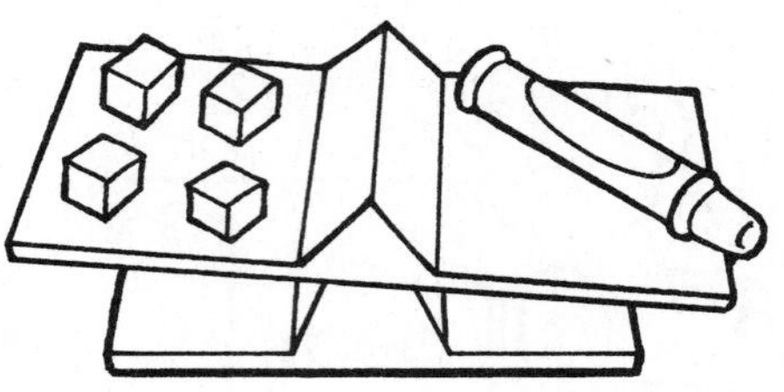

Marc has a pencil. Rob has a marker. Which object is heavier?

1. About how many ☐ will it take to balance the scale? Look at the picture. Make a prediction.

about ______ ☐ about ______ ☐

2. Measure each object to check.

about ______ ☐ about ______ ☐

3. Which is heavier? ______________________

First, make a prediction.
Then, measure to check.

4. Which is heavier, your sock or your shoe?

______________ ______________

5. Which is heavier, 1 quarter or 4 nickels?

______________ ______________

Name ____________________



# Measuring with Cups

Draw a picture.
Solve.

| | |
|---|---|
| 1. A small bowl holds 2 cups of rice. A large bowl holds double this amount. How many cups does the large bowl hold? <br> 4 cups | |
| 2. A carton of juice holds 4 cups. Mrs. Jones buys 2 cartons. How many cups of juice does she buy in all? <br> ______ cups | |
| 3. A blue jug holds 3 cups of milk. A red jug holds 2 cups more. How many cups does the red jug hold? <br> ______ cups | |

Mark the correct answer.

4. Which container holds about 1 cup?

Name ________________________________



# Temperature
# Hot and Cold

Draw a picture.

1. Jeff plays ball.
   He feels hot.
   Draw something cold for him to drink.

2. Sue goes sledding.
   She feels cold.
   Draw something hot for her to drink.

3. A jug holds 3 cups of cocoa.
   How many cups will 2 jugs hold?

   _____ cups

Mark the correct answer.

4. Which is hot?

○ 

○ 

○ 

5. Which is cold?

○ 

○ 

○ 

Name ____________________

LESSON 22.1

# Equal and Unequal Parts of Wholes

Draw lines to solve.

1. Kathy and Jane have an orange. They want equal parts. How should they cut the orange?

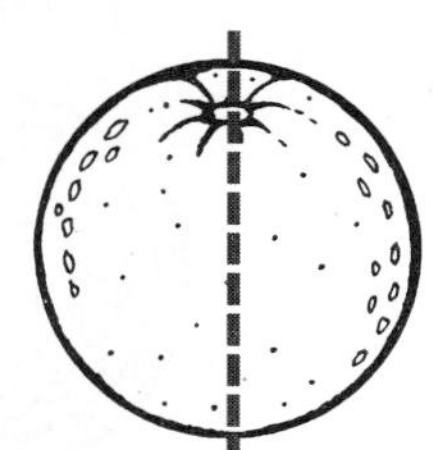

2. Sally and Tom have a sandwich. They want equal parts. How should they cut the sandwich?

3. Four children have a pizza. Each child wants an equal part. How should they cut the pizza?

4. Three children have a cake. Each child wants an equal part. How should they cut the cake?

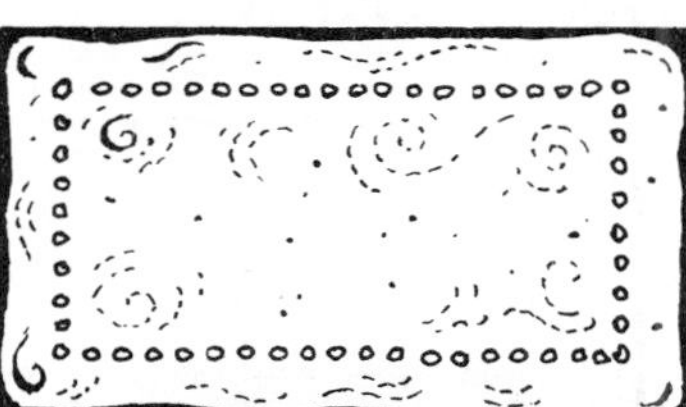

Mark the correct answer.

5. Which figure shows equal parts?

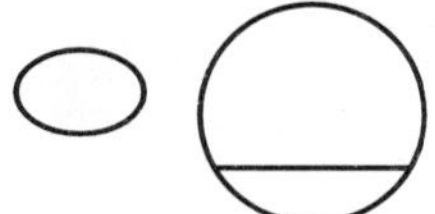

6. Which figure shows equal parts?

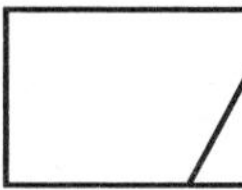

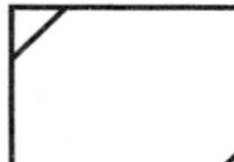

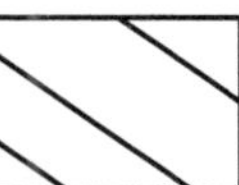

Name ______________________________



# Halves

Draw lines to solve.

1. Lily breaks a cracker to show two equal parts or $\frac{1}{2}$. Show how she could break it.

2. Bob and a friend share a pizza. Each gets $\frac{1}{2}$. Show how they could divide it.

3. Three friends have a large brownie. Each child wants an equal part. How should they cut the brownie?

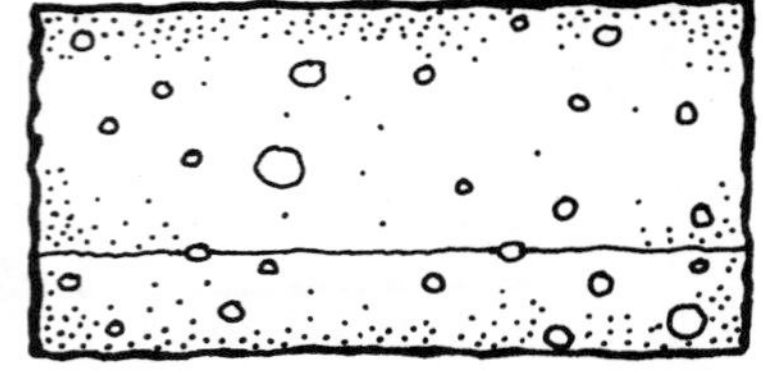

4. 4 children buy a long sandwich. Each child wants an equal part. How should they cut the sandwich?

Mark the correct answer.

5. Which figure shows halves?

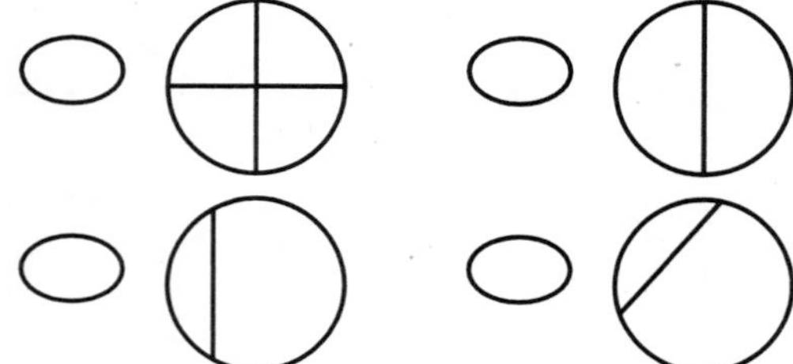

6. One of two equal parts is ____________.

◯ one half

◯ one whole

Name ____________________



# Fourths

Color the part to solve.

1. Ruth makes a sandwich. She eats $\frac{1}{4}$ for lunch. Show what part she eats.

2. Jeff's mom gives him a fruit bar. He eats $\frac{1}{2}$ for a snack. Show what part he eats.

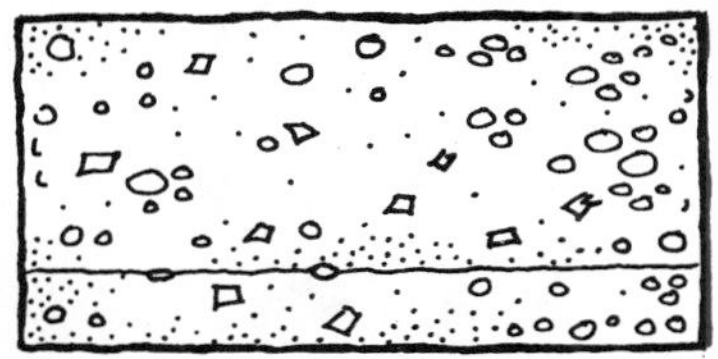

3. Peter picks an apple. He eats $\frac{1}{2}$ for dessert. Show what part he eats.

4. Mary bakes a big pizza. She gives $\frac{1}{4}$ to her friend for a treat. Show what part her friend gets.

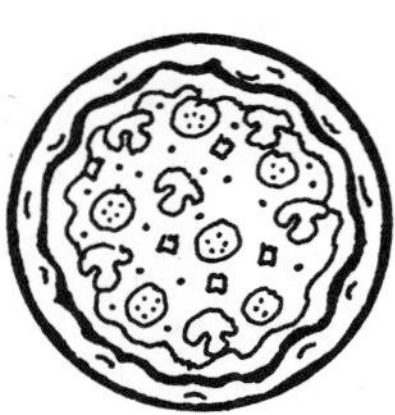

Mark the correct answer.

5. Which figure shows fourths?

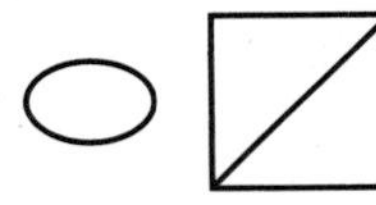
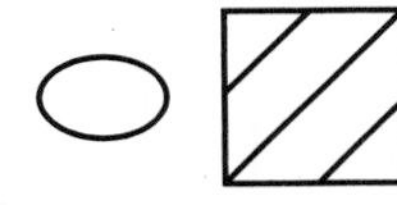

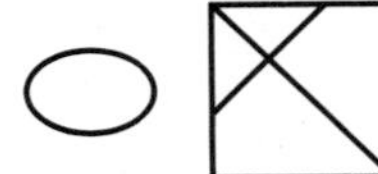

6. Which part is larger?

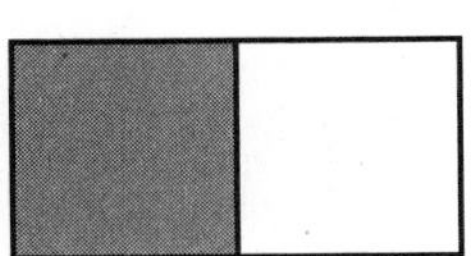
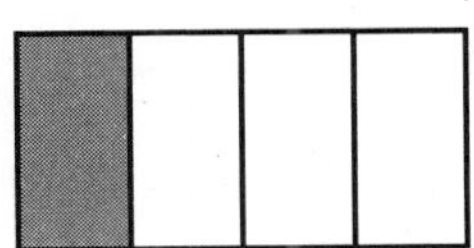

○ $\frac{1}{2}$

$\frac{1}{4}$

Name ____________________



# Thirds

Color the part to solve.

1. Toby buys a large cookie at the snack bar. He eats $\frac{1}{3}$. Show what part he eats.

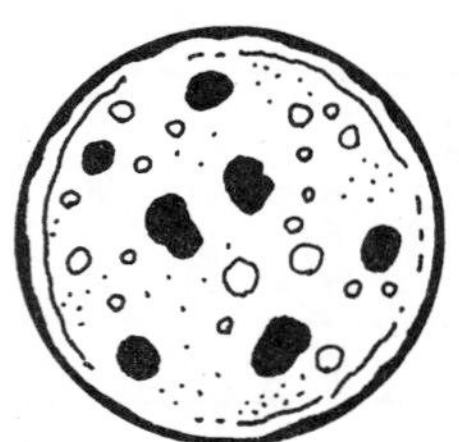

2. Sheila has a big sandwich. She gives $\frac{1}{4}$ to her brother. Show what part her brother gets.

3. Carla has a brownie in her lunchbox. She eats $\frac{1}{3}$ for lunch. Show what part she eats.

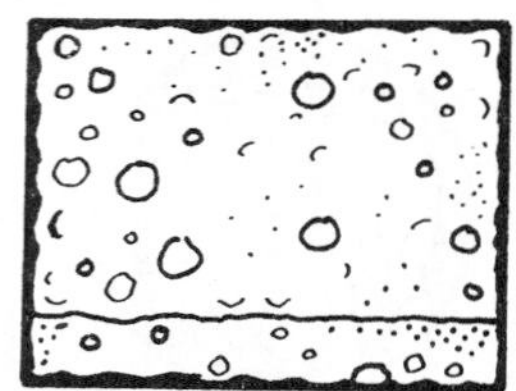

4. Garth buys a pizza. He gives $\frac{1}{2}$ to a friend. Show what part his friend gets.

Mark the correct answer.

5. Which figure shows thirds?

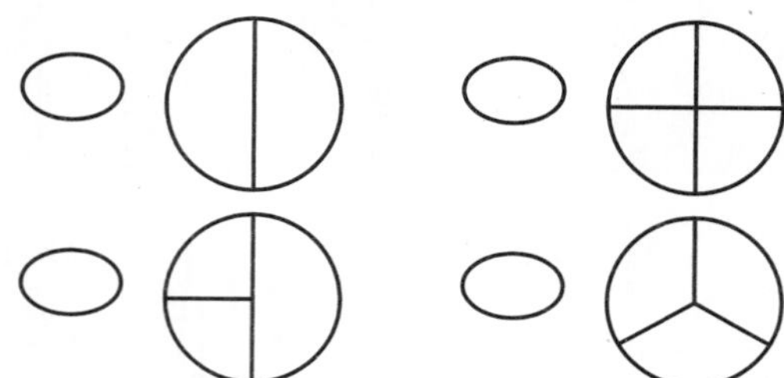

6. A pizza is cut into three equal parts. What do you call one of the equal parts?

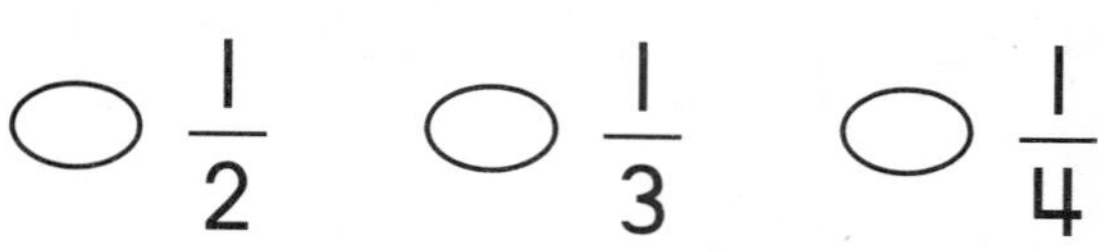

○ $\frac{1}{2}$ ○ $\frac{1}{3}$ ○ $\frac{1}{4}$

Name ________________________________________



# Reading Strategy • Use Visualization

Picturing a problem in your mind can help you solve the problem.

4 children bake a small cake.
Each child gets an equal part.
How should they cut the cake?

1. Read the problem.
   Picture the four children and the cake.

2. Then picture the cake divided into 4 equal parts.

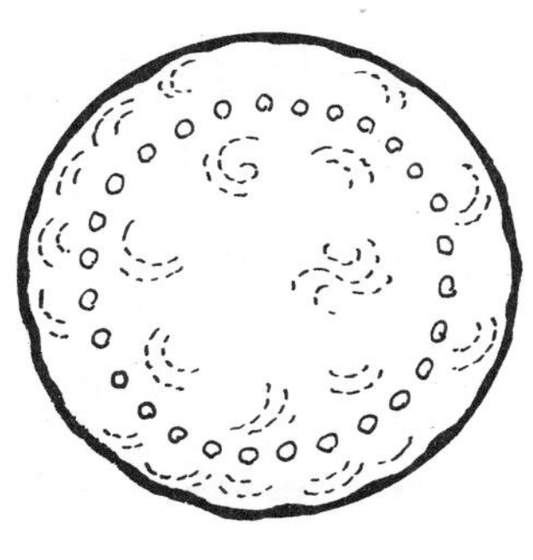

3. Draw lines on the cake to show how you pictured the cake divided into 4 equal parts.

---

Picture the problem in your mind.
Draw lines to show your picture.

4. There are 3 children in all. Each one gets an equal share of a pie. How should they cut the pie?

5. You want to share a pizza with 3 other children. How should you cut the pizza?

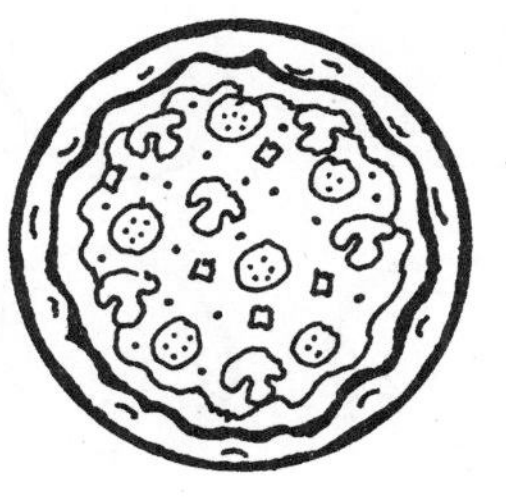

Name ____________________



# Parts of Groups

Draw and color to solve.

| | |
|---|---|
| 1. Regina has 4 toy cars.<br>1 out of 4 of the toy cars is blue.<br>Draw and color the toy cars. | |
| 2. Jose has 3 apples.<br>1 out of 3 of the apples is green.<br>Draw and color the apples. | |
| 3. There are 4 children and 1 pizza.<br>Each child gets an equal share.<br>Draw the pizza. | |

Mark the correct answer.

4. Which picture shows 1 out of 2 of the plums colored?

5. Which picture shows 1 out of 4 of the berries colored?

Name ______________________________

LESSON 23.1

# Sort and Classify

Use the table to solve these problems.

| Birds at the Feeder | |
|---|---|
| blue jay | \|\|\|\| |
| cardinal | ~~\|\|\|\|~~ \| |
| bluebird | \|\| |

1. How many blue jays did Ann see at the feeder?

   4 blue jays

2. What kind of bird did Ann see most often at the feeder?

   ______________________

3. How many birds with blue feathers did Ann see at the feeder?

   ______ birds with blue feathers

4. How would Ann show that another blue jay came to the feeder?

   ______

Mark the correct answer.

5. Which one shows the number 10?

   ○ ~~\|\|\|\|~~ \|\|
   ○ ~~\|\|\|\|~~ \|\|\|
   ○ ~~\|\|\|\|~~ \|\|\|\|
   ○ ~~\|\|\|\|~~ ~~\|\|\|\|~~

6. How are the birds in Ann's table sorted?

   ○ by age
   ○ by color
   ○ by kind
   ○ by size

Name ___________________________________



# Certain or Impossible

Use the picture.
Color the answer
to each question.

1. Sam is hungry. What can he eat from his bag?

2. Sam wants to buy a snack. What can he use from his bag?

3. Sam wants to color a picture. What can he use from his bag?

4. Sam needs to write. What can he use from his bag?

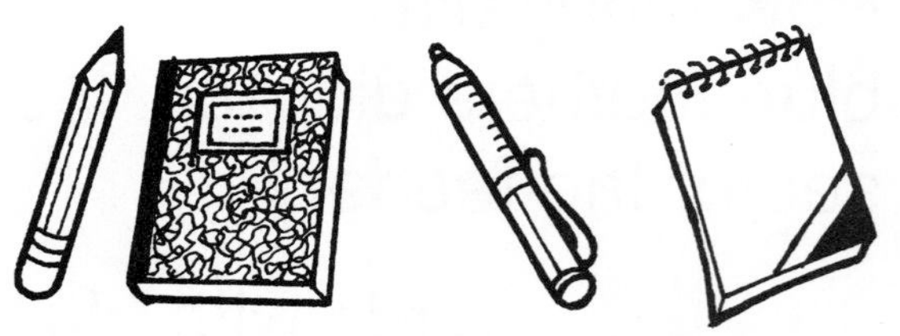

Mark the correct answer.

5. Which of these things is Sam **certain** to find in his bag?

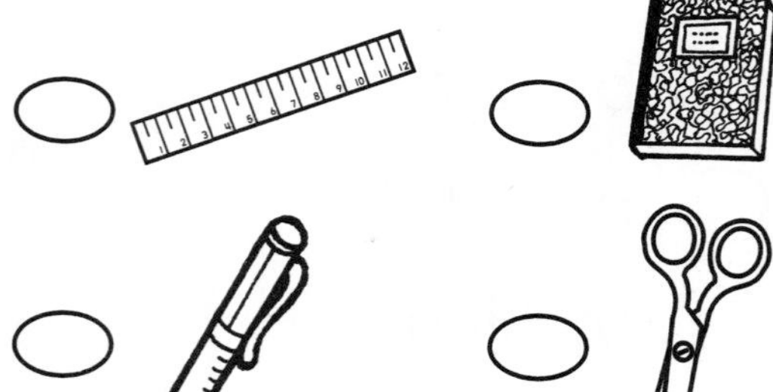

6. Which of these things is it **impossible** for Sam to find in his bag?

Name ____________________



# Most Likely

Draw a picture.
Write the answer.

1. A bag has 6 apples and 2 oranges. Jane closes her eyes and takes out a fruit. Which fruit is she most likely to get?

apple

2. A bag has green grapes and red grapes. Holly wants purple grapes. Can Holly get purple grapes from the bag?

____________________

Mark the correct answer.

3. What is your prediction for choosing a cube?

◯ impossible

◯ certain

4. What is your prediction for choosing a pyramid?

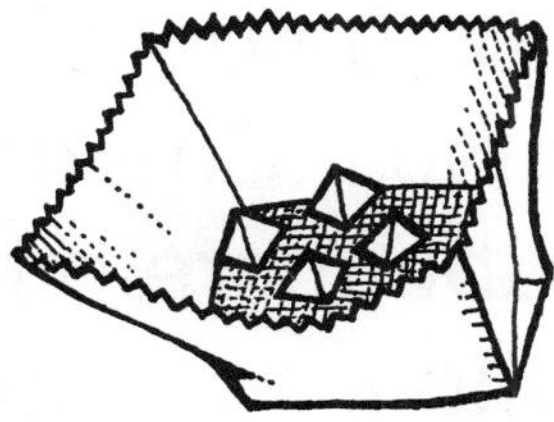

◯ impossible

◯ certain

Name ________________________________



# Reading Strategy • Use Graphic Aids

You can use a table to help you solve the problem.

Nicky has a spinner. She predicts the spinner will stop on blue more times than red.

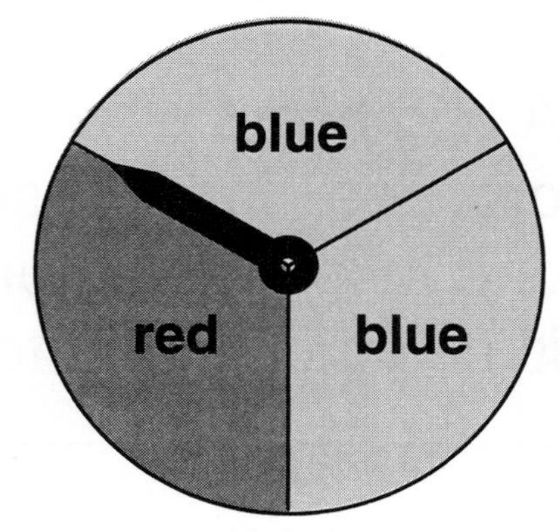


1. Which color do you predict the spinner will stop on more often?

______________________

2. When Nicky spins, she lands on blue 7 times and on red 3 times. Make a tally mark on the table for each spin. Write the totals. Check Nicky's prediction.

| | Tally Marks | Total |
|---|---|---|
| **blue** | | |
| **red** | | |

Solve.

3. Tonia has a bag with 4 red cubes and 8 white cubes. She predicts she will get a white cube more often than a red cube. When she tries, she gets red 2 times and white 8 times. Is her prediction a good one?

◯ yes ◯ no

Name ____________________

LESSON 24.1

# Picture Graphs

| Favorite Pets | | | | | |
|---|---|---|---|---|---|
| dog | | | | | |
| bird | | | | | |
| fish | | | | | |
| cat | | | | | |

Use the graph to answer the questions.

1. How many children in the class choose fish as their favorite pet?

   __3__ children

2. Write a number sentence that tells how many children like fish and birds best.

   ____ ◯ ____ = ____

3. 4 more children choose birds as their favorite pet. How many children like birds now?

   ____ children

4. The children who like cats and dogs best work together to make a picture. How many children work on the picture?

   ____ children

5. Which pet do most children like best?

   ◯ dog
   ◯ cat
   ◯ fish
   ◯ bird

6. How many children in the class like mice best?

   ◯ 5 children
   ◯ 2 children
   ◯ 1 child
   ◯ not here

Name ______________________________



# Reading Strategy • Compare and Contrast

Ramon makes a graph to find out which fruit his friends like best.

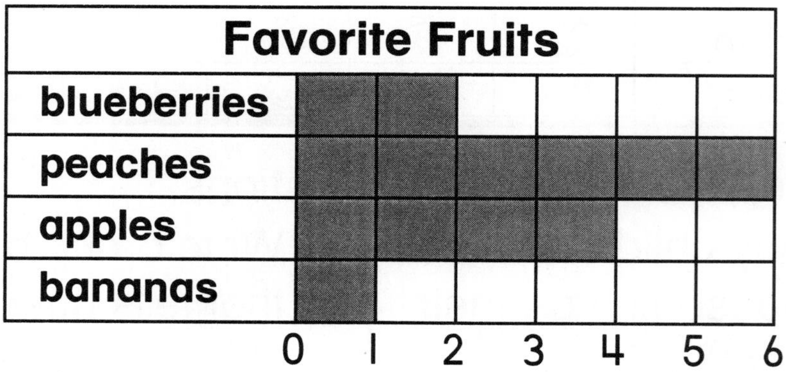

| Favorite Fruits | | | | | | |
|---|---|---|---|---|---|---|
| blueberries | ■ | ■ | | | | |
| peaches | ■ | ■ | ■ | ■ | ■ | ■ |
| apples | ■ | ■ | ■ | ■ | | |
| bananas | ■ | | | | | |
| | 0–1 | 1–2 | 2–3 | 3–4 | 4–5 | 5–6 |

1. Look at the graph.
   Compare the colored squares in each row.
   Which fruit has the most colored squares?

   ______________________________

2. Which kind of fruit do most children like best?

   ______________________________

3. Which kind of fruit do the fewest children like?

   ______________________________

4. Do more children like apples or blueberries?

   ______________________________

Name ________________________________



# Vertical Bar Graphs

1. Color the graph to match the tally table.

| Favorite Colors | | Total |
|---|---|---|
| Green | \|\| | 2 |
| Red | \|\|\| | 3 |
| Blue | \| | 1 |

**Favorite Colors**

| | Green | Red | Blue |
|---|---|---|---|
| 3 | | | |
| 2 | | | |
| 1 | | | |
| 0 | | | |

2. Which color do most children like best?

red

3. How many more children like green better than blue?

_____ child

4. How many children like red and blue?

_____ children

5. Which color did the fewest children like?

______________________

Mark the correct answer.

6. Which number sentence shows how many more children liked red than blue?

○ 3 − 1 = 2

○ 3 − 2 = 1

○ 2 + 1 = 3

7. How many children in all named their favorite colors?

○ 4 children

○ 5 children

○ 6 children

○ not here

Name ______________________________

LESSON 24.4

# Reading Strategy • Use Graphic Aids

Nancy flips a coin 10 times. She shows what happens in a tally table. Then she makes a graph to show which side of the coin turns up more often.

| Nancy's Coin Flips | |
|---|---|
| heads | |||| |
| tails | 卌 | |

1. Look at the tally table. Count the tally marks and write the totals.

| Nancy's Coin Flips | | Total |
|---|---|---|
| heads | |||| | 4 |
| tails | 卌 | | 6 |

2. Color the graph to match the tally table.

| Nancy's Coin Flips | | | | | | |
|---|---|---|---|---|---|---|
| heads | | | | | | |
| tails | | | | | | |
| | 0 1 | 2 | 3 | 4 | 5 | 6 |

Mark the correct answer.

3. Which side of the coin turned up more often?

◯ tails

◯ heads

4. Do you think that tails will always turn up more often than heads?

◯ yes

◯ no

Name ______________________________

LESSON 25.1

# Doubles Plus One

Draw a picture. Write the sums.

1. There are 6 bluebirds sitting on a fence. Then 7 more join them. How many bluebirds are there in all?

   6 + 7 = 13 bluebirds

2. There are 8 crows eating corn. Then 9 more crows come. How many crows are there in all?

   _____ + _____ = _____ crows

3. Tim draws 5 birds. Sue draws 6 more birds. How many birds do the children draw in all?

   _____ + _____ = _____ birds

Mark the correct answer.

4. Which doubles fact can help you solve

   4 + 3 = _____?

   ◯ 4 + 4  ◯ 5 + 5
   ◯ 7 + 7  ◯ 8 + 8

5. Which doubles fact can help you solve

   8 + 9 = _____?

   ◯ 5 + 5  ◯ 6 + 6
   ◯ 7 + 7  ◯ 8 + 8

Name ______________________________



# Doubles Minus One

Draw a picture. Write the sums.

1. Mrs. Park has 7 stamps. She buys 6 more. How many stamps does she have in all?

   7 + 6 = 13 stamps

2. Leroy mails 5 letters in the morning and 7 letters in the afternoon. How many letters does he mail in all?

   ____ + ____ = ____ letters

3. Mr. Jones buys 9 baseball stamps and 8 basketball stamps. How many stamps does he buy in all?

   ____ + ____ = ____ stamps

Mark the correct answer.

4. Which doubles fact can help you solve

   5 + 4 = ____?

   ◯ 3 + 3 ◯ 5 + 5
   ◯ 7 + 7 ◯ 8 + 8

5. Which doubles fact can help you solve

   8 + 7 = ____?

   ◯ 6 + 6 ◯ 9 + 9
   ◯ 8 + 8 ◯ not here

Name ______________________________



# Doubles Patterns

Draw a picture. Solve.

1. A basketball team has 5 players. Two teams meet for a game, but 1 player does not come. How many players are there?

   9 players

2. Two baseball teams play a game. Each team has 8 players. One team has 1 extra player. How many players are there in all?

   ______ players

3. A soccer team has 7 players. Two teams play a game. 1 player has to go home. How many players are left?

   ______ players

Mark the correct answer.

4. Which is a doubles-minus-one fact?
   - ◯ 9 + 9 = 18
   - ◯ 9 + 7 = 16
   - ◯ 9 + 8 = 17
   - ◯ 9 + 10 = 19

5. Which is a doubles-plus-one fact?
   - ◯ 4 + 4 = 8
   - ◯ 5 + 5 = 10
   - ◯ 5 + 4 = 9
   - ◯ 5 + 6 = 11

Name ______________________



# Doubles Fact Families

Draw a picture.
Add or subtract to solve.

1. Steve had 18 marbles. He lost 9. How many marbles does he have left?

   9 marbles

2. Cindy has 8 rocks. She finds 7 more. How many rocks does she have in all?

   _____ rocks

3. Joe finds 8 shells. Larry finds two times as many as Joe. How many shells does Larry find?

   _____ shells

Mark the correct answer.

4. Which group of three numbers can be used to make a doubles fact family?

   ◯ 4, 4, 8 ◯ 4, 6, 8
   ◯ 2, 4, 6 ◯ 4, 8, 12

5. Which number sentence belongs in a doubles fact family?

   ◯ $6 + 8 = 14$
   ◯ $7 + 7 = 14$
   ◯ $14 - 6 = 8$
   ◯ $14 - 8 = 6$

Name ______________________________



# Reading Strategy • Use Word Clues

Sal has 3 pencil toppers. Nora has **two times** as many. How many pencil toppers do they have **in all**?

Ken had 16 animal erasers. He **gave some away**. He has 8 left. How many did he **give away**?

1. Read each problem. Look for word clues. Think. How do these words help me decide if I should add or subtract?

2. Use counters to solve each problem. Draw them. Write the answers.

_____ pencil toppers

_____ animal erasers

Solve.

3. Jeff has 5 yo-yos. Noah has 1 more than Jeff. How many yo-yos do the boys have in all?

_____ yo-yos

4. Margie had 17 stickers. She gave some away. She has 9 left. How many did she give away?

_____ stickers

Name ______________________________



# Make a 10

Use the make-a-ten strategy to add.
Draw a picture.

| | |
|---|---|
| 1. Ricky has 8 baseball cards. He buys 2 more. How many cards does he have in all?<br><br>10 cards | |
| 2. Sally has 7 jacks. She finds 5 more. How many jacks does she have in all?<br><br>_____ jacks | |
| 3. Carl has 9 stickers. His sister gives him 4 more. How many stickers does he have in all?<br><br>_____ stickers | |

Mark the correct answer.

4. Which fact belongs with these facts?

   $2 + 8 \quad 6 + 4 \quad 5 + 5$

   ◯ 4 + 5 ◯ 8 + 1

   ◯ 7 + 3 ◯ 9 + 3

5. Which shows how to use the make-a-ten strategy to add 6 + 5?

   ◯ 10 + 1 = 11

   ◯ 5 + 6 = 11

   ◯ 5 + 5 + 1 = 11

Name ______________________________

LESSON 26.2

# Adding Three Numbers

Write a number sentence.
Solve.

1. Liz has 8 red beads, 8 green beads, and 1 yellow bead. How many beads does she have in all?

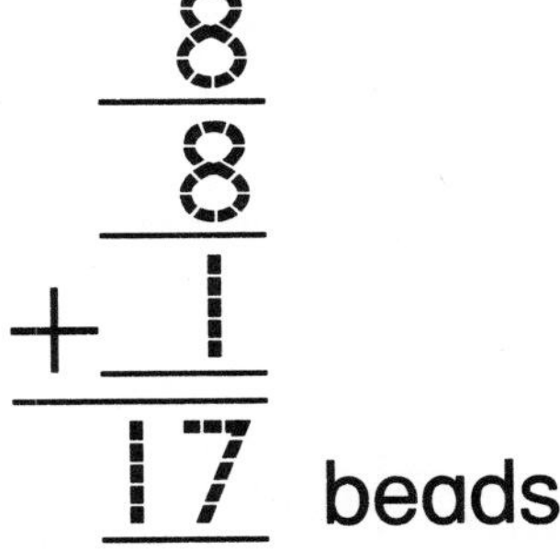

beads

2. Jim has 1 blue marble, 2 green marbles, and 9 red marbles. How many marbles does he have in all?

____
____
+ ____
____ marbles

Mark the correct answer.

3. Which strategy would you use to find this sum?

5 + 6 + 4 = ______

- ◯ doubles
- ◯ make a ten
- ◯ count on 3

4. Which problem can you use a doubles strategy to solve?

- ◯ 6 + 6 + 5
- ◯ 6 + 5 + 4
- ◯ 6 + 7 + 8

Name ________________________

LESSON 26.3

# Sums and Differences to 14

Draw a picture.
Solve.

1. Randy has 8 puppets. He gets 3 more for his birthday. How many puppets does he have in all?

   __11__ puppets

2. Randy has 11 puppets. He leaves 3 at school. How many puppets does he have now?

   ______ puppets

3. Jane has 7 yellow trolls, 2 red trolls, and 5 green trolls. How many trolls does she have in all?

   ______ trolls

Mark the correct answer.

4. Which subtraction sentence is related to this addition sentence?

   $7 + 9 = 16$

   ◯ $16 - 8 = 8$
   ◯ $16 - 7 = 9$
   ◯ $9 - 7 = 2$

5. Which three numbers could be used to make related addition and subtraction sentences?

   ◯ 5, 8, 13
   ◯ 6, 9, 12
   ◯ 7, 5, 11

Name ______________________________

LESSON 26.4

# Sums and Differences to 18

Draw a picture to solve.

1. There are 8 children at the playground. 9 more children come. How many children are at the playground?

   17 children

2. 3 children ride bikes. 5 children play on the slide. 7 children swing. How many children are playing in all?

   ______ children

3. There are 17 children at the playground. 8 go home for lunch. How many children are left?

   ______ children

Mark the correct answer.

4. Which strategy could you use to solve this problem?

   $6 + 7 =$ ______

   ◯ doubles

   ◯ make-a-ten

   ◯ doubles plus one

5. What subtraction fact can you figure out by knowing

   $8 + 7 = 15$?

   ◯ $15 - 10 = 5$

   ◯ $15 - 7 = 8$

   ◯ $15 - 9 = 6$

Name ______________________________



# Counting Equal Groups

Draw a picture.
Write how many in all.

| | |
|---|---|
| 1. Mrs. Jones has 4 window boxes. She plants 3 flowers in each box. How many flowers in all? <br> 12 flowers | |
| 2. Mr. Hill has 3 pots. He plants 3 seeds in each pot. How many seeds in all? <br> ______ seeds | |
| 3. Ms. Green has 5 plants. Each plant has 2 flowers. How many flowers in all? <br> ______ flowers | |

Mark the correct answer.

4. Which picture shows 2 groups of 3?

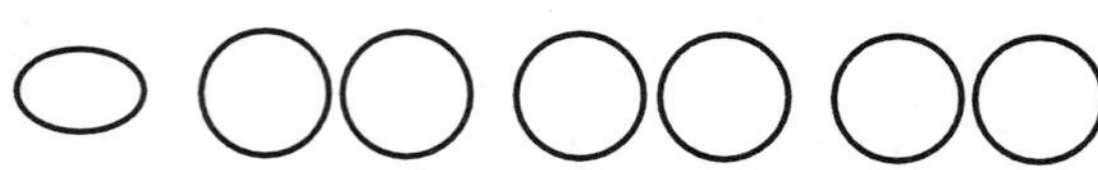

○ not here

5. Which addition sentence shows 3 groups of 4?

○ $4 + 3 = 7$

○ $4 + 4 + 4 = 12$

○ $3 + 3 + 3 + 3 = 12$

○ not here

Name ______________________________



# How Many in Each Group?

Draw a picture.
Solve.

1. Larry feeds 9 bananas to 3 monkeys. Each monkey gets the same number of bananas. How many bananas does each monkey get?

   3 bananas

2. Pam feeds 12 fish to 4 seals. Each seal gets the same number of fish. How many fish does each seal get?

   ______ fish

3. Larry feeds 3 goats. He gives them 4 cups of food each. How many cups of food does Larry need?

   ______ cups

Mark the correct answer.

4. Which is greater?

   ◯ 3 groups of 4

   ◯ 3 groups of 3

5. Which has more groups?

   ◯ 2 groups of 5

   ◯ 5 groups of 2

Name ____________________

LESSON 27.3

# How Many Groups?

Draw a picture.
Solve.

1. Art has 12 rolls. He puts 6 rolls in each basket. How many baskets does he use?

2 baskets

2. Noah has 3 friends. He gives them each 3 crackers. How many crackers does he need?

____ crackers

3. Trudy has 8 cookies. She puts 2 cookies on each plate. How many plates does she use?

____ plates

Mark the correct answer.

4. Which picture shows 4 groups of 3?

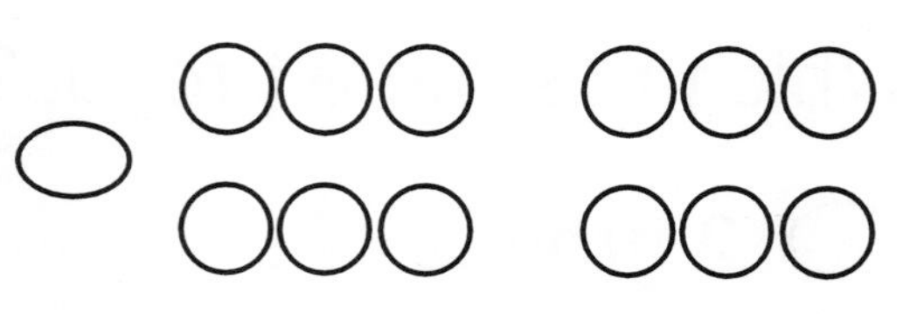

not here

5. Which addition sentence shows adding 3 groups of 5?

$3 + 5 = 8$

$5 + 5 + 5 = 15$

$3 + 3 + 3 + 3 + 3 = 15$

Name ______________________________

LESSON 27.4

# Reading Strategy • Use Word Clues

Using word clues can help you solve problems.

| There are **3 bowls** of fruit salad. **Each bowl has 2** red grapes. How many red grapes **in all**? | There are **12 cherries** and **3 bowls**. How many cherries **in each bowl**? | There are **15** green **grapes**. Anna put **5 grapes in each bowl**. **How many bowls** did she use? |
|---|---|---|

1. Read the problem. Look for word clues.

2. Use these word clues to help you. Draw a picture. Then solve.

6 red grapes in all

4 cherries in each bowl

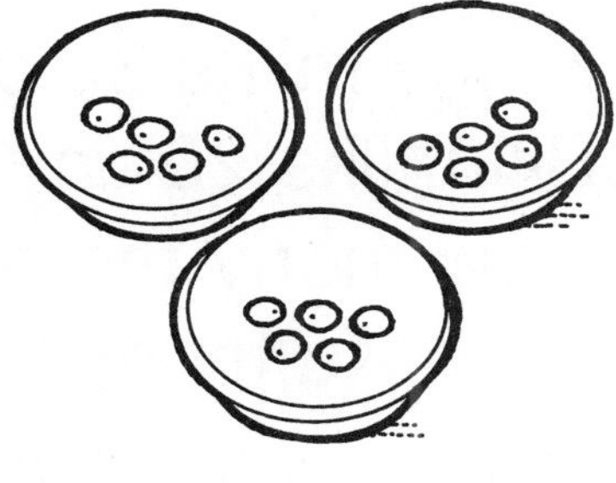

3 bowls

Solve.

3. There are 9 crackers. Each child gets 3. How many children get crackers?

_____ children

4. There are 3 children. Each child gets 2 cups of juice. How many cups of juice in all?

_____ cups of juice

Name ______________________________



# Adding and Subtracting Tens

Draw a picture.
Find the sum or difference.

1. Mr. Ellis has 50 cows. He buys 10 more. How many cows does he have in all?

60 cows

2. Mrs. Ellis has 90 blocks of cheese. She sells 20 blocks. How many blocks of cheese does she have left?

______ blocks of cheese

3. Kathy milks 30 cows. Bill milks 20 cows. How many more cows does Kathy milk?

______ more cows

Mark the correct answer.

4. Find the sum.

$$\begin{array}{r} 30 \\ +20 \\ \hline \end{array}$$

- ◯ 5
- ◯ 30
- ◯ 50
- ◯ 55

5. Find the difference.

$$\begin{array}{r} 70 \\ -60 \\ \hline \end{array}$$

- ◯ 70
- ◯ 60
- ◯ 50
- ◯ 10

Name ____________________

LESSON 28.2

# Adding Tens and Ones

Draw a picture.
Find the sum.

1. Ned spends 57¢ on a notebook and 11¢ on a pencil. How much does Ned spend in all?

   68 ¢

2. Phil has 50¢ in his pocket. He earns 20¢ more. How much money does Phil have?

   ______ ¢

3. Karen wants to buy 2 cards. Each card costs 30¢. How much money does Karen need?

   ______ ¢

Mark the correct answer.

4. Add.

| tens | ones |
|---|---|
| 5 | 2 |
| +2 | 6 |
|  |  |

- ◯ 87
- ◯ 77
- ◯ 78

5. When adding tens and ones, begin by adding the ______ first.

- ◯ ones
- ◯ tens

Name ______________________________



# Subtracting Tens and Ones

Draw a picture.
Find the sum or difference.

1. Mrs. Jones makes 46 cookies. She gives 12 cookies to Tim and his friends. How many cookies are left?

   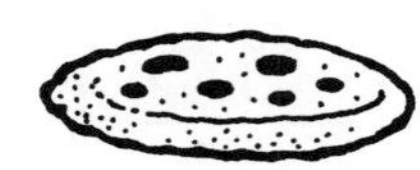

   34 cookies

2. The Cub Scouts make 20 tacos. They eat 10 for lunch. How many tacos are left?

   ______ tacos

3. Mary makes 24 trail mix bars. Paula makes 24 also. How many trail mix bars do they make?

   ______ trail mix bars

Mark the correct answer.

4. Subtract.

| tens | ones |
|---|---|
| 4 | 5 |
| −3 | 1 |
| | |

○ 76

○ 41

○ 14

5. When subtracting tens and ones, begin by subtracting the ______ first.

○ ones ○ tens

Name ________________________________

LESSON 28.4

# Reading Strategy • Use Word Clues

Using word clues can help you decide if an answer to a problem makes sense.

José has **61 shells.**
He finds **12 more.**
How many shells does he have in all?

7 shells 73 shells 730 shells

1. Read the problem. Look for word and number clues to help you find the answer that makes sense.

2. Decide if the answer is likely to be in the ones, tens, or hundreds.

3. Choose the answer that makes sense.

_____ shells

Mark the answer that makes sense.

4. Mr. Williams has 47 stamps. He uses 42. How many stamps does he have left?

○ 5 stamps
○ 89 stamps
○ 500 stamps

5. Alice has 53 marbles. She buys 35 more. How many marbles she have now?

○ 88 marbles
○ 880 marbles
○ 22 marbles